Second Edition

English for Adult Competency

BOOK 2

OBSOLETE

Autumn Keltner
Gretchen Bitterlin

SAN DIEGO COMMUNITY COLLEGE DISTRICT

PRENTICE HALL REGENTS
Englewood Cliffs, New Jersey 07632

Editorial/production supervision and
 interior design: Noël Vreeland Carter
Manufacturing buyer: Ray Keating
Cover design: Bruce Kenselaar

Illustrated by Mark Neyndorff

Printed in the United States of America

10 9 8 7 6 5 4 3 2

ISBN 0-13-280355-0

Prentice-Hall International (UK) Limited, *London*
Prentice-Hall of Australia Pty. Limited, *Sydney*
Prentice-Hall Canada Inc., *Toronto*
Prentice-Hall Hispanoamericana, S.A., *Mexico*
Prentice-Hall of India Private Limited, *New Delhi*
Prentice-Hall of Japan, Inc., *Tokyo*
Simon & Schuster Asia Pte. Ltd., *Singapore*
Editora Prentice-Hall do Brasil, Ltda., *Rio de Janeiro*

CONTENTS

INTRODUCTION   vii

1 PERSONAL IDENTIFICATION AND SOCIAL COMMUNICATION   1

Topics: Personal information, introductions, polite expressions, time, telephone communication

Functions: Requesting and giving information, expressing and responding to greetings and polite expressions, clarifying, apologizing, asking for permission

Structures: WH questions, prepositions of location, present perfect, present perfect continuous, modal would (polite requests), embedded questions, modals may and can (permission), can (ability)

Life Skill Reading: Telephone bill

2 FOOD AND MONEY   25

Topics: Comparison shopping, complaints, recipes, prices and change, measurement, eating out

Functions: Comparing prices and quality, expressing needs and preferences, expressing dissatisfaction, requesting, reporting and interpreting information, expressing obligation, correcting

Structures: WH questions, comparatives and superlatives, there is/are, some/any, much/many, and little/few with count and noncount nouns, modals would, could, should, may, have to, perfect modal must have, past tense (regular verbs), partitives

Life Skill Reading: Recipe, food store ad, soup label, menu

3 HEALTH CARE 48

Topics: Childhood illnesses, reporting an absence from school, immunizations, obtaining medical care and medications, emergencies, making an appointment, communicating with a doctor or dentist

Functions: Requesting and giving information, reading and interpreting information, describing a situation, asking for and giving advice, reporting information

Structures: Present perfect with since/for, ever/never, already/yet, just, present perfect passive, clauses of time with before, after, when, while, future tense going to, reported speech (affirmative and negative statements, imperatives), modals have to, could (possibility, permission, past ability), should (advice), might (possibility), causal have (passive), past progressive with while, gerunds and infinitives

Life Skill Reading: Immunization chart, health history form, medicine labels, medical warnings

4 TRANSPORTATION 72

Topics: Street and freeway directions/location, traveling by bus, car purchase and maintenance, driver's license, traffic tickets, accidents, insurance

Functions: Requesting and reporting information, reading and interpreting information, describing problems/situations, making excuses, requesting clarification, expressing desire, expressing intention, warning

Structures: Embedded questions, prepositions of location, WH questions, clauses of time with before, after, when, until, imperatives, present real conditional, modals might, would, infinitives, either/or, past progressive with when, causals have, get

Life Skill Reading: Bus schedule, gasoline pump instructions, car ads, driver's license application, instructions in the event of an accident

5   HOUSING   96

Topics: Obtaining housing, interacting with neighbors, tenant rules and responsibilities, maintenance and repairs, telephone service

Functions: Asking for and reporting information, reading and interpreting information, requesting, complaining, apologizing, describing problems/situations, expressing obligation, requesting permission, expressing needs and desires, insisting

Structures: Reported speech, passive voice (present, past), WH questions, yes/no questions, modals may, could (permission, polite requests), can (permission, ability), must, have to, clauses with unless, present real conditional, present perfect with since/for, causals have, get, reflexive pronouns

Life Skill Reading: Housing ads, tenant rules, rental application, insecticide label

6   SHOPPING AND BANKING   113

Topics: Buying clothes, clothing care instructions, exchanges, layaway purchases, cashing a check, overdrawn account, charge account, opening a savings account, garage sale

Functions: Complimenting, describing, making comparisons, expressing preferences, expressing dissatisfaction

Structures: Tag questions, adjective phrases, adjective clauses, comparisons with as. . .as, present real conditional, present unreal conditional, negative questions, supposed to, adverbs

Life Skill Reading: Clothing labels, newspaper ad, checking account deposit slip

7   EMPLOYMENT: GETTING AND KEEPING A JOB   129

Topics: Looking for a job, job training, job ads, job interview, talking with co-workers and supervisors, reporting work progress, calling in sick, locating tools, asking for a promotion

Functions: Offering suggestions, requesting and giving information, initiating a conversation, requesting clarification, expressing future intentions, responding to criticism

Structures: Present perfect, present perfect continuous, reported speech (commands, statements, questions), WH questions, used to, gerunds, adverb clauses, prepositions of location, present real conditional, embedded questions, modals would, could (polite questions)

Life Skill Reading: Job ads, job application form

8 COMMUNITY RESOURCES 156

Topics: Tracing a lost package, registering and insuring mail, postage rates, arranging for day care, parent-teacher conference, library card, weather forecast, recreation, TV and movie schedules, reading the newspaper, community resources

Functions: Requesting and giving information, describing problems, expressing possibility, stating intentions, giving advice, expressing obligation

Structures: Modals in the past, passive voice with modals, adverb clauses, phrases with except, separable two-word verbs, present unreal conditional, gerund with two-part verbs (interested in going)

Life Skill Reading: Postal rate charts, package label, TV schedule, movie schedule, newspaper index, community resource directory

9 GOVERNMENT AND LAW 178

Topics: Consumer contract, Legal Aid, small claims court, rights when arrested, types of courts and crimes, citizenship, Bill of Rights, government agencies, levels of government

Functions: Describing problems, requesting assistance, complaining, insisting, reporting information, requesting clarification, expressing congratulations, expressing necessity, asking for and giving advice, stating intentions, expressing obligation

Structures: Reported speech, embedded clauses, present real conditional, modal should, gerund with two-part verbs, noun clauses, passive voice, present unreal conditional, modal must

Life Skill Reading: Citizenship information, list of government agencies

APPENDIX 201

Supplementary Activities

Index of Grammar Structures

INTRODUCTION

English for Adult Competency, Books 1 and 2 are basic texts for adult students who need to learn the oral language patterns and vocabulary required in day-to-day situations. They provide classroom teachers with materials that are effective and relevant to the real needs of non- and limited-English speaking adults.

Book 2, intended for students who have had at least one year of instruction in English as a Second language, consists of nine units.

    I.   Personal Identification and Social Communication
   II.   Food and Money
  III.   Health Care
   IV.   Transportation
    V.   Housing
   VI.   Shopping / Banking
  VII.   Employment
 VIII.   Community Resources
   IX.   Government and Law

The content of the units in *Book 2* is similar to the content in *Book 1*. However, *Book 1* is not necessarily a prerequisite for success in *Book 2*. The purpose of the materials in *Book 2* is to reinforce and expand the basic concepts, vocabulary, and structures introduced at the beginning level of instruction. The topics in each unit are developed in greater depth, with more complex grammatical structures, functions, and vocabulary. The goal of instruction in *Book 2* is that the student apply a knowledge of the English language and communications skills to the topic areas in order to deal effectively with adult activities.

The units are situation-oriented, non-sequential, and minimally structured. Each unit is independent and can be used separately in whatever order best meets the students' needs.

Each unit consists of the following:

1. A list of competency objectives
2. A student needs assessment exercise
3. Situational or functional dialogues
4. Vocabulary and structure practices
5. Interactive pair practice exercises
6. Visuals
7. Interview questions
8. A life skill reading exercise

The performance-based objectives, listed on the first page of each unit, designate functional competencies that students are to achieve. Since the text is designed primarily to develop oral communication skills, demonstrated performance of the competency objectives is stressed. Structures are focused on in the pattern practices following the dialogues. Structural patterns are presented as they appear in the dialogues, not in any particular order. Not all structure items usually suggested for the intermediate level of English have been included in these units. What has been attempted is to present a basic program to cover the most common language patterns which develop communicative competence in English, enabling adults to function successfully in the daily situations which they are most likely to encounter.

In addition to structures, language functions, such as requesting clarification, requesting and reporting information, and making introductions, are also addressed where applicable. At the intermediate level, it is beneficial to teach the students a variety of ways a message can be communicated, rather than just one way. For example, in making introductions, it is possible to use various forms based on the degree of formality required. The practices and pair practice exercises in each chapter provide the opportunity for students to use different expressions to communicate similar ideas.

Teaching Guidelines

It is strongly recommended that the teacher read through and study each unit before beginning instruction. By so doing the teacher will have a clear idea of the scope of the unit, its goals and objectives, and the activities which draw on students' experiences and introduce, reinforce, and lead to mastery of the concepts.

NEEDS ASSESSMENT EXERCISES   Two types of student needs assessments are included: (1) an overall text needs assessment and (2) individual needs assessments for each unit in the text.

It is suggested that instructors administer the general needs assessment prior to beginning the text and each unit needs assessment prior to beginning the specific unit. The tendency of most ESL students is to check all competencies or topics, feeling that they want or need to learn everything. Instructors might suggest options such as (1) having students prioritize the items in each category by marking their highest priority needs as one, the next "two," and so forth, or (2) limiting the number of items students can check in each category.

Use of these needs assessments will assist instructors in determining which units, and which competencies within units, to stress and give more time and which might be omitted or given less time. Thus, students are given an opportunity to provide input as to where they want or need to interact in English and instructors are able to provide a curriculum that is immediately relevant to their students' needs and goals.

DIALOGUES   The structural patterns and concepts of each unit are introduced through dialogues which center around a single situational topic. The following steps are recommended in the presentation of a dialogue:

1. *SETTING THE SCENE*   Before presenting the dialogue itself, it is important to set the scene or provide a meaningful context for the dialogue. The teacher can prepare the students by using the visuals in the text to generate a discussion of what the dialogue might be about and what language might be used. The teacher should elicit as much information as possible from the students in order to determine their previous knowledge and experience with the content. The teacher may also describe the situation presented through the dialogue, using the vocabulary necessary for comprehension of the dialogue. By pre-teaching the core vocabulary and expressions, the students will be better prepared to comprehend the dialogue in context.

2. *LISTENING COMPREHENSION*   Once the scene is set, the teacher models the dialogue with books closed. The teacher uses pictures, gestures, pantomime, or whatever is necessary to get the meaning across. If an aide is available, teacher and aide may each take a part. Following the modeling, the teacher asks different types of questions (yes/no questions, WH questions, etc) to check comprehension of the dialogue.

3. *REPETITION OF THE DIALOGUE*   Once the students demonstrate an understanding of the dialogue, the teacher models each line of the dialogue and the students repeat. With complex patterns and longer utterances, the teacher may elicit repetition phrase by phrase, starting from the end of the utterance (This is called a backward build up repetition drill). This practice is more productive with books closed because the purpose of the repetition is to practice pronunciation and intonation of the utterances. If students are reading the lines of the dialogue, they cannot focus on the appropriate intonation required. When students have repeated each line after the teacher, the teacher takes one role (A) and the students take the other (B). The students may have their books open during this step. Then the students and teacher change roles and repeat again. Next the teacher divides the class in half. One half assumes one role, the second half, the other. The roles can then be changed again. Finally, pairs of students may practice the dialogue with each other, while the teacher circulates, listening for pronunciation problems or other difficulties.

4. *PRACTICE OF THE DIALOGUE*   On subsequent days, further practice of the dialogue can be accomplished in small groups or pairs with students alternately acting out the various roles. Rather than reading the dialogue each time, students should begin generating the lines of the dialogue with minimal cues. The teacher can write the first few words of each line of the dialogue on the board and facilitate practice of the dialogue in this way on subsequent days.

    Dialogues are not necessarily designed for memorization. They are instead a device for developing language structure, topical vocabulary, and concepts. The sentences in the dialogue serve as models for practicing and expanding the language and cultural context of the topic. The final and most crucial step is for the students to reconstruct the dialogue using their own words or adaptations to communicate in a relevant, real-life situation.

PRACTICES   A series of substitution drills usually follows each dialogue. They are intended to be meaningful and communicative, not merely mechanical. These exercises serve two basic purposes. First, they are designed to reinforce the structure patterns and vocabulary introduced in the dialogues. Second, through substitutions using pertinent topical vocabulary, they serve to expand the basic concepts of the unit. In these drills, students focus on substituting one word in the model sentence (noun replaced by another noun, verb by another verb, etc.) or focus on substituting a phrase for another phrase that communicates the same message. A substitution drill can be cued with spoken words, concrete objects, pictures, or written words. Concrete objects and visuals used to cue the drills make the drills more meaningful.

Example: Teacher: What's your zip code?
           Students: What's your zip code?
           Teacher: What's your zip code? (his)
           Students: What's his zip code?
           Teacher: What's his zip code? (her) (etc.)

It is extremely important and necessary for the teacher to repeat the correct response after the students have said it. This provides the positive reinforcement needed for mastery. Since the emphasis in this text is on the functional, oral use of English, grammatical labels and explanations have been avoided. The structure points of each lesson are practiced in exercises which require the student to concentrate on meaning, listening and reacting to what is being said and using the language, not just learning about it.

VISUALS   Visuals are an integral part of each unit. These adult-oriented pictures and charts add realism and relevance when used to do the following:

1. Set the scene for the situations in the dialogues. By asking questions related to the visuals, the teacher can assess how relevant the situation is to the students' lives and how much language they already have to communicate in that situation.
2. Develop the topic concepts for each unit.
3. Evaluate student mastery of structure, content, vocabulary, and concepts. The visuals used in the pair practices serve as cues for the students to generate the language patterns they have previously learned in the dialogues.
4. Relate to similar experiences in the students' own lives. Visuals stimulate students to talk about their own experiences.

Each full page visual is usually accompanied by a structured communicative exercise to allow for practice of specific language patterns related to the visual.

PAIR PRACTICE ACTIVITIES   Pair practice activities include the following types of exercises:

1. Substitution dialogues—Students practice a dialogue (usually similar to the model dialogue), substituting new words or phrases each time. (See example on page 8)
2. Cued dialogues—Only a few words or cues are given for each line of a previously modeled dialogue. Students reconstruct the dialogues in conversations with each other. (See example on page 35)
3. Incomplete dialogues—Students practice a previously modeled dialogue by seeing only the first words of each line. Students complete the dialogue lines in order to carry out the conversation. (See example on page 15).
4. Chain/extension drills—A student asks another student a previously modeled question and in response to his answer must ask another spontaneous question to continue the conversation.
5. Charts—Students use cues or grids to ask and answer questions of each other. (See more detailed section on charts)
6. Information Gap Activities—Students take turns asking questions to get information they don't have in order to complete the exercise. One student always has the information that the other doesn't have. (See more detailed section on information gap activities)

The following steps are recommended in order to conduct pair practice activities in the classroom:

1. Model the example for the students, choosing a way to indicate two people are talking. If necessary, ask questions to check comprehension of the language and concepts used in the pair practice.
2. Practice the model with the whole class, the teacher taking one role and the class, the other.
3. Change roles and practice with the whole class again.
4. When the students demonstrate that they have control of the language required in the pair practice and that they understand the task, divide the class into pairs.

5. Ask one pair of students to model the task for the whole class, using the first substitution or example.

6. Direct the students to practice in pairs, constantly circulating among them to monitor their progress. Remember that the focus of these activities is communication. Keep error correction to a minimum or this communication will be inhibited. Make mental note of problem areas for total class practice later.

7. Bring the class together and practice with the whole class as needed to review pronunciation patterns, structural patterns, or vocabulary items that might still be difficult for the students. You may want to ask a few volunteers to perform the task in front of the class to culminate the pair practice activity.

INFORMATION GAP ACTIVITIES   The difference between traditional pair practice activities and information gap activities is that in pair practice activities both students have the same information; they are simply practicing known, predictable questions and responses. In information gap activities, each partner has different information students must communicate in order to complete a task using visuals, grids, or charts. This type of pair practice is obviously more challenging because if the communication is not clear, the task cannot be completed. The steps for information gap activities are the same as those for pair practice except that in information gap activities, students should not look at each other's papers. Sometimes standing a manila folder up between students' materials creates a good barrier to enforce the information gap or students can sit back to back to minimize the likelihood of students looking at one another's materials. When students realize that they cannot look at another's paper, they are more likely to listen more attentively to each other and request clarification many times if necessary to complete their task.

CHARTS OR GRIDS   Charts or grids enable students to practice asking each other questions with minimal prompts. Although there isn't much to read on a chart, reading a grid is in itself a skill that must be taught. The following steps are recommended: (See page 51 for example)

1. The instructor models all questions and answers on the grid for the whole class, pointing to the cues on the grid.

2. The instructor asks each question on the grid. Students respond as a whole group.

3. The instructor and students change roles. Students ask the instructor the questions; the instructor responds.

4. The instructor chooses a student in the class to question for the ''you'' section. The instructor asks the student the questions; the instructor writes in the student's responses.

5. The instructor divides the class into pairs.

6. The instructor selects one pair of students to model the questions and answers for the rest of the class.

7. As the students practice with each other, the instructor circulates among the students to monitor their progess.

8. As needed, practice again with the whole class.

9. As a culminating activity or a review on subsequent days, create a blank grid on the board with the same categories and complete the ''you'' section for several students in the class by having students ask a volunteer student all the questions on the grid.

To elicit the best results from using charts, the teacher should not write out the questions for the students; instead, students should only use the cue words to generate their questions and answers.

Grids can be more communicative by also being information gap exercises. In these exercises, students follow the same steps but must fill in information on their grids as they ask the necessary questions. (See the phone bill information gap/grid activity on page 22.)

INTERVIEW QUESTIONS   Many units in the text include one or more interview activities. These activities are designed to assist students in using previously practiced language and concepts in less controlled situations. Students use the language for the purpose of obtaining real information from their partner(s) and later share this information with the rest of the class.

The first student asks the questions and another responds. The first student listens carefully, asks for repetition or clarification if necessary and takes notes to assist in sharing the information at the conclusion of the activity. Then roles are reversed and student two asks the questions.

To prepare students for this type of activity, the instructor should first model each question, have students repeat, and check comprehension. If additional preparation is needed, the instructor can ask a student volunteer each question and/or volunteers can ask the instructor the questions. Then pairs or small groups practice while the instructor circulates, provides assistance if needed, and identifies problem areas for total class practice later. The final step is for students to report back, sharing and discussing the information they have obtained. If desired, students' responses may be used to develop a chart or grid for further practice and reenforcement.

PICTURE SEQUENCES   Several of the units include picture sequences, a series of four visuals designed to progressively illustrate a situation or problem. (See page 16). While the focus of the sequences is the development of oral language skills, they can also be used to practice writing skills.

The picture sequences can be used in various types of activities. The first step in any case is to develop the vocabulary and concepts. As much as possible, this content should be elicited from the students. In some cases, key questions or vocabulary are provided beneath the visuals as cues.

Steps to follow may include:

1. Look at each picture in sequence. Elicit and/or provide key vocabulary, identify actions, describe and discuss the situation, answer the question(s) provided.
2. Elicit from students' their experiences with similar situations or problems.
3. Have students retell the situation in their own words.
4. Have students in pairs or small groups create dialogues and role play for the whole class.
5. Have students match sentences with visuals and/or put sentence strips in chronological order.
6. Have students write sentences from dictation.
7. Have higher level students write paragraphs, short stories or variations of the situation while the instructor works on oral language skills with the remainder of the class.
8. Relate each situation to students' previous experiences in the U.S. or in their native countries.

READING EXERCISES   Each chapter contains at least one life skill reading exercise. The purpose of each reading selection is to expose students to the type of reading they need to do in carrying out day to day survival tasks, i.e. read a job ad or interpret a health history form. Tasks include the following types of reading: bills, forms, ads, charts, labels, schedules, instructions, menus, and directories. A comprehension exercise follows each life skill reading display, consisting of one or more of the following types of questions:

1. True/false statements
2. Open ended questions
3. Multiple choice questions patterned after the types of questions students have on standardized life skill reading tests, such as the CASAS tests administered in several states. (CASAS = Comprehensive Adult Student Assessment System)

Each set of questions includes factual, inferential, and evaluative questions in order to develop students' reading skills and critical thinking skills.

1. Factual questions include the following types of questions:
   a) Yes/no questions
   b) WH questions answerable from one part of the reading display.
   c) WH questions answerable from two different parts of the reading display.

In order to develop reading skills, it is recommended that all three types of factual questions be asked.

2. Inferential questions require students to take the information given, read between the lines, and draw conclusions based on information that is not explicitly stated.

3. Evaluative questions require the students to go beyond the reading selection and either make judgments or give opinions or apply the information to their own lives.

The following steps are recommended for presenting each reading lesson:

1. Pre-reading—Ask questions to elicit the students' experience related to the content and concepts of the life skill reading exercise. Discuss new vocabulary expressions or terms that will be needed.

2. Scanning the display—Point out the headings, titles and important sections of the display to assist the students in scanning for the information they need.

3. Ask the students a series of questions aurally to develop their listening comprehension as well as their scanning skills. To teach scanning, ask students how they found the information needed to answer the questions.

4. Follow up—Direct the students to the written questions. Do the first question or example with the students to model the procedure. When the students have finished the exercise, provide an opportunity for them to check their answers and relate the situation to their own experiences.

The most important skill in life skill reading is scanning to get the specific information that is needed. Students need to be trained not to read every word and not to look up every new word in the dictionary. When possible, encourage the students to practice guessing the meaning of new words as they appear in context.

FIND SOMEONE WHO   Unit 5 includes an example of a Find Someone Who activity. The purpose of this type of activity is to review previously learned material in an interactive mode. Students (interviewers) move around the room asking their classmates (interviewees) questions. The questions may be asked in any order. If the response to a question is "yes," the student who responded writes his or her name on the appropriate line. If the response to the question is "no," the student must continue around the room asking questions until an affirmative response is obtained. The activity continues until a student indicates that he or she has responses for all of the items listed.

Before beginning the activity, the instructor checks to be certain the students can formulate the questions needed to elicit the responses. For example, the instructor might ask, "Who can tell me the question to ask for number one?" A student volunteers, "Have you ever had your carpet cleaned?" The instructor has the total class repeat the question in unison and continues eliciting examples until certain that the students have command of the language needed to complete the activity.

Followup: The instructor calls on individual students to share the information collected and discuss the responses. Extension questions can be asked by the instructor or students e.g. "Who cleaned it?, "How much did it cost?"

This type of activity can be developed as a review or culminating activity for any unit by varying the content, vocabulary, and grammatical structures as appropriate. (See examples below)

Unit I   Find Someone Who . . . .
1. was born in Mexico. _____
2. has lived in the United States less than one month. _____
3. speaks Vietnamese. _____

Unit IV   Find Someone Who . . . .
1. knows which bus to take downtown.
2. knows where the nearest bus stop is.

3. knows how much the fare from _____ to _____ is. etc.

Depending on the needs and abilities of the students, the exercise can focus on the use of one structure only or several structures may be used in the same exercise.

Sample Competency Based Lesson Plan

CHAPTER 3

PAGES 50–53

Competency: The student will be able to report an absence from school and describe history of childhood diseases

Function: Ask for and report information

Structure focus: Present perfect tense

The following plan suggests activities over a 3-day period to allow for review and reinforcement of the new language patterns and vocabulary within the lesson. The time required for each activity would depend on the level of the students and their demonstrated performance.

DAY 1

Warm up/Review

Using the visuals on pages 52 and 55, review symptoms and illnesses with students by practicing the pattern, "What's the matter with him/her?" To introduce new vocabulary that may be needed for the new lesson, this drill can be extended as follows: "She has a rash. She might have the measles. She's coming down with the measles."

Presentation of new lesson: Reporting an absence from school—page 50

Before modeling the new dialogue, ask the students if they have children. Have they ever called their children's schools to report an illness? Elicit from the students expressions or language patterns they might use to call the school in order to find out what vocabulary terms and language patterns they already use and what they need to learn. If the dialogue appears to be relevant after this informal needs assessment, continue with steps 1–4. (See Introduction for detailed information on teaching a dialogue).

1. Teacher models the dialogue. Students listen
2. Teacher asks comprehension questions to check that students understand the dialogue.
3. Teacher may discuss new vocabulary and idioms that come up in the dialogue.
4. Teacher and students practice each line of the dialogue, changing roles. (see suggested steps in teacher's guide)

Practice

1. Teacher conducts the drills in the "practice section" as needed.
2. *Pair practice:* (p. 50) This can be done on day 1 or held until day 2.
   a. Teacher models the short dialogue in the pair practice.
   b. Teacher practices the first example with the whole class, changing roles.
   c. Teacher divides the class into pairs and circulates among them as they practice the dialogue making the necessary substitutions.
   d. Teacher reviews pair practice dialogue again with the whole class, if needed.

DAY 2

Review of dialogue: Reporting an absence from school

1. Teacher writes the dialogue on page 50 on the board, leaving periodic blank spaces (close exercise); then elicits from the class the appropriate words for the blank spaces

or

The teacher writes the first few words of each line as cues for the students to re-generate the dialogue learned the previous day.

Example: A. My son

B. What seems

A. He has _____ I think

B. What grade

A. _____

B. Who's

A. _____

B. OK Thanks for

2. Additional group repetition of the dialogue should be elicited if students need it. (Dialogue will be new for those who were absent or are new students).

3. Teacher asks for volunteers to do dialogue, making substitutions practiced the previous day in the pair practice.

4. Teacher models small group practice on page 50 and circulates among groups to listen to students.

New lesson: **Pair practice with chart on page 51**

1. *Warm-up:* Ask students if they have had the measles or chicken pox. Model the pattern, "Have you ever had _____ ?" Conduct a chain drill around the room, allowing students to practice this pattern, recording the answers on the board as follows:

	measles	chicken pox
Name _____	no	yes

Conduct additional drill, focusing on the present perfect tense, as needed.

2. Refer the students to the chart on page 51. Model the questions and answers and practice with the whole class first. (See steps on working with "grids.")

3. Have students practice in pairs and circulate to see how students perform.

DAY 3

1. Review the dialogue "reporting an absence from school" again in a less structured format than on days 1 and 2. Either put fewer cues on the board or ask students to volunteer to role play the dialogue, given new vocabulary (i.e. Jane, mumps, 6th grade).

2. Conduct drills again with the pattern "Have you ever had _____ ?"

3. Model and facilitate the pair practice on the bottom of page 51.

4. Interview Questions: (Page 52) Discuss these questions with the whole class or have students sit in groups of 4 and discuss with each other. To culminate the activity, ask a representative of each group to share the information arrived at.

Reading Exercise: "Immunization Record"

1. Discuss the concept of immunization as a pre-reading activity. Point out major headings on the chart to help the students learn how to scan for information.

2. Model the activity of reading the question, looking at the chart and then selecting the best answer for the question. Do #1 together with the class.
3. After students complete the reading activity on their own, correct the answers together with them.
4. As a follow up activity, ask students to bring in their children's immunization records if they have them. Students can then question each other on the dates of specific immunizations.

NOTE: For a lower level class or for a class that meets in a shorter time period, the above sequence might take up to 5 days.

According to the needs of the students, an instructor may also want to include other activities related to this lesson plan such as:

- more extensive structure practice
- more pronunciation exercises
- jazz chants
- songs
- supplementary writing practice

NAME _____

1. **The most important reason I am studying English is to**

   _____ get a job; get a better job; go to job training.

   _____ get more education (high school, college, other).

   _____ take care of myself and my family's needs.

   _____ become a citizen of the U.S.

   _____ other _____ .

2. I speak English most often when I

   _____ talk with my friends.   _____ talk to my neighbors.

   _____ use the telephone.   _____ take care of my house.

   _____ buy food at the market.   _____ shop for clothing.

   _____ order meals in a restaurant.   _____ talk with people at a bank.

   _____ talk to doctors or nurses.   _____ talk to people at work.

   _____ talk to a dentist.   _____ talk with my children's teachers.

   _____ ask for information.   _____ talk with my landlord.

   _____ ask for directions.   _____ need help at the post office.

   _____ need services for my car.   _____ need other services.

   _____ ride a bus.   _____ other _____ .

3. I need to read English better to

   _____ read the newspaper.   _____ fill out forms.

   _____ understand housing ads.   _____ read housing agreements.

   _____ understand job ads.   _____ understand bus schedules.

   _____ understand food or clothing ads.   _____ read labels on clothing, food, or medicine.

   _____ use a telephone book.   _____ other _____ .

4. I need special help with _____ .

chapter 1

PERSONAL IDENTIFICATION AND SOCIAL COMMUNICATION

COMPETENCY OBJECTIVES

On completion of this chapter the students will show orally, in writing, or through demonstration that they are able to use language needed in the following situations:

A. PERSONAL INFORMATION

- Give, on request, self-identification and personal information, including name, address, telephone number, date and place of birth, age, Social Security number, nationality, marital status, previous education, and occupation.
- Fill out a personal information form.

B. TIME

- Ask for and tell the time in minutes and hours.

C. INTRODUCTIONS AND POLITE EXPRESSIONS

- Give and respond to common greetings.
- Make and respond to simple introductions.
- Use and respond to polite expressions.

D. TELEPHONE COMMUNICATION

- Answer incoming calls and take simple messages.
- Respond appropriately when making or receiving a wrong-number call.
- Use directory assistance to obtain a telephone number.
- Report a telephone out of order.
- Utilize the telephone and telephone directory to make all types of local and long-distance calls.
- Read and interpret a telephone bill.

NEEDS ASSESSMENT EXERCISE

PERSONAL IDENTIFICATION AND SOCIAL COMMUNICATION

I need to improve my English so that I can

_____ answer questions about myself and my family.

_____ fill out a personal information form.

_____ ask for and tell the time in hours and minutes.

_____ use and respond to common greetings.

_____ introduce people.

_____ use and respond to polite expressions (apologize, compliment).

_____ answer the telephone and take messages.

_____ know what to do and say if I get a wrong number on the phone.

_____ use directory assistance to get a telephone number I don't know.

_____ use the telephone and telephone directory to make local and long-distance telephone calls.

_____ report that a telephone is out of order.

_____ read and understand my telephone bills.

PERSONAL INFORMATION

A: May I help you?
B: Yes. I'd like to enroll in an English class.
A: OK. What's your name, please?
B: Carlos Gomez.
A: Your first name again?
B: Carlos.
A: How do you spell that?
B: C-A-R-L-O-S.
A: OK. Where are you from, Carlos?
B: I'm from Mexico.
A: How long have you been here?
B: About four months.
A: What was your occupation before you came here?
B: I was a carpenter.
A: Do you have a job now?
B: No. Not yet.
A: How many years of school did you finish in your country.
B: Five years.
A: Thank you. Please fill out the rest of this form and take it to room 210.

Below is a credit application form. It asks for other types of personal information. Talk about the form with your teacher and class and then complete the form.

APPLICANT

FULL NAME	☐Married ☐Unmarried ☐Separated	NO OF DEPENDENTS (INCL. APPLICANT(S))	SOCIAL SECURITY NUMBER	DRIVER'S LICENSE NO	BIRTHDATE Mo/Day/Yr
SPOUSE'S NAME (FULL NAME)			SPOUSE'S SOCIAL SECURITY NO	SPOUSE'S BIRTHDATE Mo/Day/Yr	
HOME ADDRESS	CITY/STATE		ZIP	HOME TELEPHONE NO	HOW LONG? YRS MO
PREVIOUS ADDRESS	CITY/STATE			ZIP	HOW LONG? YRS MO
NEAREST RELATIVE NOT LIVING WITH YOU		COMPLETE ADDRESS		RELATIONSHIP	
EMPLOYER	ADDRESS/CITY		PHONE NO	OCCUPATION	HOW LONG? YRS MO
PREVIOUS EMPLOYER (IF NOT WITH CURRENT EMPLOYER FOR 2 YRS)	ADDRESS/CITY			OCCUPATION	HOW LONG? YRS MO

PRACTICE

What's your name?
        address?
        zip code?
        telephone number?
        area code?
        Social Security number?

What's your place of birth?
        country of origin?

What's your date of birth?
        birthdate?

Where are you from?   Where were you born?
    is   she   was she
       he   he

When were you born?
What year were you born?
      day

Where do you live?
        study English?
        work?

I live in San Diego.
      New York.

I live near Hoover High School.
      Balboa Park.

I live on Ulric Street.
      Redding Road.

I live at 665 Lake Street.
      2256 Green Drive.

What was your occupation before you came here?
What did you do?
What was your job?

I was a welder.
      a secretary.
      a police officer.
      an engineer.

How long have you been here?
                lived here?
                studied English?

Please fill out this form.
      complete
      review
      sign
      check over

Pair Practice: Practice with your class. Then sit in pairs and ask each other questions that go with the pictures. Write the answers down so that you can tell about your partner later.

EXAMPLE: Student A: What's your name?
          Student B: (answers the question)

When you finish, take turns describing your partner to the class.

EXAMPLE: Student A: My partner, Maria Gomez, lives at 350 Elm St. Her zip code is 92106. Her telephone number is 453-8732. Her Social Security number is 564-83-3647. She is from Mexico. Her birthday is June 5. She is married. She is a student.

Pair Practice: Practice with your class. Then sit in pairs and ask each other questions about the people listed on the chart.

	Where	How long	What language	What
Carlos	Mexico	2 months	Spanish	mechanic
Anh	Vietnam	6 months	Vietnamese	nurse
Som	Laos	1 1/2 years	Laotian	soldier
Chou	Laos	3 months	Hmong	farmer
Navid	Iran	2 years	Farsi	teacher
You	——	——	——	——

EXAMPLE: Student A: Where is Carlos from?
          B: He is from Mexico.
          A: How long has he been here?
          B: He has been here for two months.
          A: What language does he speak?
          B: He speaks Spanish.
          A: What was his job in Mexico?
          B: He was a mechanic.

INTERVIEW

1. Where are you from?
2. How long have you been in the United States?
3. When did you leave your country?
4. Did you come here alone?
5. Why did you leave your country?
6. How did you leave?
7. Did you have any problems?
8. How long did it take to come to the United States from your country?
9. Where did you go first when you arrived in the United States?
10. What do you like here?
11. What don't you like here?
12. Do you miss your country sometimes?
13. What do you miss?
14. What do you think is the most difficult problem in coming to a new country?

GREETINGS

A: Hello, Maria.
B: Hi, how have you been?
A: Fine, thanks. How about you?
B: OK. I haven't seen you in a long time. What have you been doing?
A: I've been studying a lot. Did you hear about my brother, John?
B: No, what happened?
A: He and Ann got married last month.
B: Really? That's great. Tell them I said hello.
A: I will. I've got to go or I'll be late for class. Give me a call sometime.
B: I'll do that. See you later.

PRACTICE

How have you been?
           they
           the children
  has he
           she
           your mother

What have you been doing?
                  up to?

I've been busy.
         tired.
She's sick.

I've been working.
         learning English.
         studying electronics.
She's been looking for a job.

That's great.
That's too bad.
Congratulations!
You're kidding.
Really!
Have a good time.
I'm sorry to hear that.

Small Group Practice: Sit in groups of four and ask each other the following questions.

How have you been?
What have you been doing?

Student 1 asks student 2. Student 2 answers and asks student 3. Student 3 answers and asks student 4.

Pair Practice: Sit in pairs and practice the dialogue with the new words (marked 1, 2). For the last substitution (3), choose the best response from all those listed at the bottom of the page. Practice with the class before you practice with your partner.

A: Hi _____ . What's new?

B: Did you hear about $\underset{1}{\underline{Mary}}$?

A: No. What happened?

B: $\underset{2}{\underline{\text{She passed the driving test}}}$.

A: $\underset{3}{\underline{\text{That's great!}}}$

1. Mary
2. passed driving test

3. _____

1. Paul
2. failed driving test

3. _____

1. John and me
2. got married

3. _____

1. me

2. going to France next week

3. _____

1. Ann
2. had car accident

3. _____

1. Jack
2. won $100 in the lottery

3. _____

1. Jim
2. mother died

3. _____

1. _____

2. _____

3. _____

3. That's great!
   That's too bad.
   Congratulations!
   You're kidding.
   Really!
   Have a good time.
   I'm sorry to hear that.

INTRODUCTIONS AND FAMILY

Ali: Jose, I'd like you to meet my friend, Minh. Minh, this is Jose.
Jose: Hello, it's nice to meet you.
Minh: Glad to meet you, too. Ali has told me a lot about you.
Jose: That's nice to hear.

PRACTICE

I'd like you to meet my friend.
                         husband.
                         wife.
                         father-in-law.
                         sister-in-law.
                         cousin.
                         niece.
                         nephew.

FORMAL: I would like to introduce you to _____ .

I would like you to meet _____ .

I want you to meet _____ .

Have you met _____ ?

Do you know _____ ?

INFORMAL: This is _____ .

FORMAL: I am pleased to meet you.
It's a pleasure meeting you.
It's nice to meet you.
I'm happy to meet you.
I'm glad to meet you.
It's good to meet you.
INFORMAL: Nice to meet you.

What is the best thing to say?

Thank you.
Excuse me./Pardon me.
My pleasure.
I'm very sorry.
You're welcome.
That's OK.

Read the situation that goes with each picture. Look at each picture and decide what the person should say. Choose from the examples below or suggest other expressions.

Picture 1: You bump into somebody.
2: Somebody is in the way. You want to go through the door.
3: You need to leave the dinner table.
4a: You step on somebody's toe.
4b: Somebody steps on your toe and apologizes.
5: You sneeze near somebody.
6: Somebody compliments you.
7: Somebody gives you a gift.
8: Somebody thanks you for taking her to dinner.
9: You want to interrupt two people who are talking.

TELLING TIME

A: Excuse me. Do you have the time?
B: Yes, it's 5 after 2.
           10 past 2.
           a quarter past 2.
           20 past 2.
           half-past 2.
           20 to 6.
           a quarter to 6.
           10 to 6.
           a few minutes before 6.
           a few minutes after 2.

A: Can you tell me what time it is?
B: I'm sorry, I can't. My watch is broken.
                            slow.
                            fast.

PRACTICE

Can you tell me   What time is it?
                       what time it is?

Can you tell me   How much is it?
                       how much it is?

Can you tell me   Where is it?
                       where it is?

Can you tell me   When is it?
                       when it is?

Pair Practice: Sit in pairs and ask each other the following questions. Begin each question with "Can you tell me?" or "Do you know?".

EXAMPLE: Student A: Can you tell me what time it is?

                Student B: It's _____ .

1. What time is it?
2. What is your zip code?
3. What is the date?
4. What is your address?
5. What is your teacher's name?
6. Where is the office?
7. Where is the nearest pay phone?
8. Where is the nearest bus stop?
9. Where are the restrooms?

10. Where _____ ?

TAKING A MESSAGE

A: May I speak to Bill?
B: I'm sorry. He's not home now.
A: Do you know when he'll be back?
B: No, I don't.
A: Would you please give him a message?
B: Just a minute, I have to get a pencil.
   OK. Go ahead.
A: Would you please ask him to call John at
   7:00 this evening? My number is 263-7753.
B: OK. I'll leave him the message.
A: Thanks a lot.

PRACTICE

May I speak to Bill?
Can
Could

He's not here.
         home.
    out right now.

Do you know when he will be back?
                         come?
                         pick me up?
                         be free?

Would you please give him a message?
                take a message?
                hold the line?
                try again later?
                repeat that?

Would you please ask him to call John?
                        pick me up?
                        call me back at 10:00?
                        return my call?

Would you please have him call John?
                        come to my house?
                        meet me at school?
                        call me back at 10:00?

WOULD YOU LIKE TO LEAVE A MESSAGE? _____

Pair Practice: Practice these conversations with your teacher and then with a partner. Use the substitutions in 1, 2, and 3 in each of the numbered blank spaces. When you finish, make up some examples of your own to share with the rest of the class.

A: Is Tam Lee there?

B: No, he isn't. He's _____ .
$$1$$

A: Do you know when he'll be back?

B: Not until _____ . Would you like to leave a message?
$$2$$

A: Yes, tell him _____ / _____ .
$$3$$

B: O.K. I'll give him the message.

1. at school right now	1. out of town
2. about 6	2. tomorrow afternoon
3. Ric called/I'll call back about 8	3. Dr. Brown's office called/He has an appointment at 9 Wednesday morning
1. working late tonight	1. next door
2. after 10	2. after dinner
3. Jo called/I'll bring his papers by about 7:30 in the morning	3. Colorcam called/His pictures are ready
1. at Kim's soccer game	1. at a movie
2. about 4	2. very late
3. Bill called/I'll pick him up about 7	3. Tim phoned/The boss wants him to come in an hour early tomorrow

Pair Practice: Take turns listening to the phone messages below. Write down who and when to call and the telephone number. If you are student A, cover the student B side. If you are student B, cover the student A side. First student A asks the question and then student B.

EXAMPLE 1:   Student A: May I take a message?

Student B: Yes. Please tell John to call <u>Mary</u> at <u>8:30 P.M.</u> at
                                                         1   2

<u>265-7530</u> .
       3

Student A: (Writes message in blanks)

EXAMPLE 2:   Student B: May I take a message?

Student A	*Student B*
Call _____	**1.** Mary
Time _____	**2.** 8:30 P.M.
Number _____	**3.** 265-7530
1. Dr. Brown	Call _____
2. 9:00 tomorrow	Time _____
3. 223-1040	Number _____
Call _____	**1.** Frank
Time _____	**2.** After 10 tonight
Number _____	**3.** 459-2966
1. Sally	Call _____
2. 5:15	Time _____
3. 230-0042	Number _____

WRONG NUMBER

A: May I speak to Joe Smith?
B: No one by that name lives here. What number are you calling?
A: I'm calling 275-2063.
B: I'm sorry. You have the wrong number.
A: Oh, excuse me. Sorry to bother you.
B: That's all right.

PRACTICE

I'm sorry. You have the wrong number.
                                person.

Sorry to bother you.
        disturb you.
        wake you up.
        trouble you.

Pair Practice: Sit in pairs and role-play the following conversation with your partner.

A: May I speak to _____ ?

B: No one _____ .

    What number _____ ?

A: I am calling _____ .

B: I'm afraid _____ .

A: Sorry to _____ .

1. What did he do first?

2. Do you think he reached the right person? Why? Why not?

3. What did he do next? Who answered the telephone? Was the person at home? Where was he?

4. What did she do next?

Small Group Practice: Talk about the pictures with your class. Then sit with two other students. Decide what each person in pictures 2, 3, and 4 is saying, and then practice the conversation. Share your conversation with the rest of the class.

PICTURE 2

    Student A: _____

    Student B: _____

PICTURE 3

    Student A: _____

    Student C: _____

PICTURE 4

    Student A: _____

    Student C: _____

TELEPHONE INFORMATION

A: John, I wonder what happened to Ann Lee. I haven't heard from her in a long time.
B: Didn't she move to Arizona?
A: Yes, but I have no idea how to reach her. I've lost her phone number and address.
B: Why don't you call directory assistance in Phoenix?
A: How do I do that?
B: It's simple. Just dial 1 plus the area code plus 555-1212.
A: Do you know the area code?
B: No, I don't. But you can find it in the phone book.
A: Thanks, I'll look it up. She may not be listed, but it's worth a try.

PRACTICE

I wonder what happened to Ann Lee.
                              my old friend.
                 time he'll be home.
            why he is late.
            where the phone book is.
            where the keys are.

I have no idea how to reach her.
                       call her.
                       get in touch with her.
                       phone her.

Didn't she move to Arizona?
            get a job?
            change her phone number?
            leave a forwarding address?
            get in touch with you?

Why don't you call directory assistance?
                     look in the yellow pages?
                     look it up in the directory?

DIRECTORY ASSISTANCE

A: Directory assistance for what city?
B: San Diego.
A: Go ahead.
B: Do you have a number for William Parks?
A: Spell the last name, please.
B: P-A-R-K-S.
A: B-A-R-K-S?
B: No. *P* as in *paper*.
A: I have a William Parks on Pine Street.
B: Yes. That's right.
A: The number is 292-1485.

INTERVIEW

1. Have you ever called directory assistance? Why did you call?
2. Did you get the number you wanted?
3. Did you have any problems?

Class Discussion: Think of words for the following letters that can be used to clarify spelling. Write the words in the blanks.

1. *B* as in _____

2. *L* as in _____

3. *R* as in _____

4. *V* as in _____

5. *H* as in _____

6. *T* as in _____

7. *Z* as in _____

8. *G* as in _____

9. *K* as in _____

10. *A* as in _____

11. *E* as in _____

12. *I* as in _____

Pair Practice: Sit in pairs and practice the "Directory Assistance" conversation above using other names instead of William Parks. When necessary, use the words in the blanks above, or other words you can think of to clarify spelling.

PAY PHONE—COLLECT CALL

Jose and Kim were traveling to Los Angeles by car when their car broke down on the freeway. They found a pay phone, but a call to their friend in Los Angeles would be long distance, and they didn't have enough change to pay for the call.

A: Look, Jose, there's a pay phone. Let's call John and ask him to help us.

B: But it's long distance, and I don't have that much change.

A: Just call collect.

B: How do I do that?

A: Deposit your money, wait for the dial tone, and then dial 0 plus the area code (213) plus his number.

B: OK. Here goes!

Operator: Operator.

B: I'd like to make a collect call.

Operator: Your name, please?

B: Jose Gomez.

C: Hello.

Operator: I have a collect call from Jose Gomez. Will you accept the charges?

C: Yes, I will.

B: Hi, John. I'm sorry I called collect, but our car just broke down, and I'm out of money and stranded on the freeway.

C: Where are you?

B: About half an hour from you, on highway 5 north.

C: Don't worry, I'll be right there. Tell me exactly where you are.

INTERVIEW

1. Have you ever called collect?
2. Who did you call?
3. Why did you call collect?
4. Did you have any problems?

Small Group Practice: Sit in groups of three and role-play the following conversation.

A: I'd like to make a collect call.

Operator: Your name, please?

A: (Give name.)

B: Hello.

Operator: I have a _____ .

Will you _____ ?

B: _____ .

Long-Distance Dialing

Unassisted station calls	Inside area code area	Dial 1 + telephone number
	Outside area code area	Dial 1 + area code + telephone number
*Operator-assisted calls collect/credit card	Inside area code area	Dial 0 + telephone number
	Outside area code area	Dial 0 + area code + telephone number

*After you dial the number, the operator will come on the line.

Directory assistance	Inside area code area	Check your local directory.
	Outside area code area	Dial 1 + area code + 555-1212

Take-Home Assignment: At home, try to get the following information about your long-distance phone company. Then bring the information to class and share it with the other students.

1.   What long-distance company do you have?
2.   What does the company charge for directory assistance?
3.   When does the billing start on a long-distance call with your company?
4.   Choose a city that you might call. If you call during the day, what is the cost for the first minute and each additional minute?
5.   If you call the same city at night, what is the cost for the first minute and each additional minute?

LONG DISTANCE—PERSON-TO-PERSON

A: I'd like to make a person-to-person call to San Francisco.
Operator: You can dial that call direct. It's cheaper that way. Just dial 0, then the area code, and then the number.
A: Thank you. I didn't know I could do that. (Caller dials the number.)
Operator: (To person making call.) Operator.
A: I'd like to make a person-to-person call to Kim Wong.
Operator: Just a moment, please. (Telephone rings.)
B: Hello.
Operator: I have a person-to-person call for Kim Wong.
B: This is Kim Wong speaking.
Operator: Go ahead, please.

BAD CONNECTION

A: Operator, I was cut off on my call to San Francisco. Would you please put the call through again?
Operator: The number you were calling, please?
A: 415-345-3010.

PRACTICE

I'd like to make a person-to-person call to _____ .
    place a collect
        long-distance
    charge this call to my home number.
    know the time and charges of this call.

You can dial that call direct.
    charge that call to your number.
    use your telephone credit card.
    ask the Operator for assistance.
    look it up in the telephone directory.

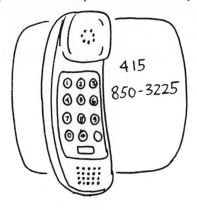

INTERVIEW

1. Have you ever called person-to-person? Why?
2. How much did it cost?

Pair Practice: Sit in pairs and ask each other questions to help you fill in the missing information on your long-distance phone bill.

SAMPLE QUESTIONS

1. When did you make the call?
2. What time did you call?
3. What city did you make the call to?
4. What number did you dial?
5. How long did you talk?
6. How much was the call?

EXAMPLE: Student A: What city did you call on October 30?
Student B: Santa Ana.
Student B: What time did you call Santa Ana on October 30?
Student A: 3:43.

ACCOUNT M6040172 INVOICE 44178771 CYCLE 11 DECEMBER 7, 1989

——— DETAIL OF MCI DIAL DIRECT CALLS ———

	DATE	TIME	TO	CALLED	MIN	$AMOUNT
Student A.	Oct. 30	3:43 P		714-973-6881		.41
	Nov. 2	2:53 P	Garden Grove		4	.57
	Nov. 18		Beverly Hills	213-277-0932	23	
	Nov. 23	2:23 P	Los Angeles		7	.93
Student B.	Oct. 30		Santa Ana	714-973-6881	1	
	Nov. 2	2:53 P		714-740-4211	4	.57
	Nov. 18	9:21 P	Beverly Hills			4.44
	Nov. 23	2:23 P	Los Angeles	213-389-9912	7	

READING A TELEPHONE BILL

To: John Brown

Account Number	619 455-0317 159 S 9	Please Save for Your Records	Page 1
		Check No.:	
Statement Date	Feb. 17, 1990	Date:	
		Amount:	

Account Summary	Previous bill	47.97	
	Payments applied through Feb. 20, 1990	47.97CR	
	Balance (thank you for your payment)		.00
	Current charges:		
	Pacific Bell (Page 2)	20.69	
	AT&T Communications (Page 4)	4.52	
	MCI (Page 5)	5.44	
	Current charges due by Mar. 17, 1990		30.65
Total Due	A late charge applies if not received by Mar. 19, 1990		30.65
Whom to Call	For billing questions call:		
	Pacific Bell	No Charge	(619) 695-5111
	AT&T Communications	No Charge	1-800-222-0300
	MCI	No Charge	(619) 695-5111
	When moving or placing an order call:		
	Pacific Bell	No Charge	(619) 695-5999

Study John Brown's telephone bill above to answer the following questions.

1. How much did he pay last month?
2. How much does he have to pay this month?
3. When does he have to pay this bill?
4. What number should he call if he doesn't understand his telephone bill?
5. If he wants to move, what number should he call?

INTERVIEW

1. Do you have a telephone in your house?
2. Who pays the phone bill in your house?
3. Have you ever found a mistake on your telephone bill? What did you do?
4. What can you do if you find a mistake on your phone bill?
5. What would you say if you found a mistake on your phone bill?

TELEPHONE REPAIR

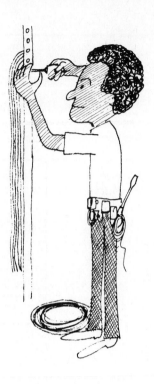

A: Telephone Repair.
B: I'd like to report a telephone out of order.
A: Your number, please?
B: 254-7369.
A: What's the problem?
B: There's no dial tone.
A: Does it ring when someone calls you?
B: No, I can't call out, and nobody can call in.
A: OK. We'll check it and get back to you. Will you be home this afternoon?
B: Yes, I will. Thank you.

PRACTICE

My phone is out of order.
         is dead.
         is disconnected.
         doesn't work.

What's the problem? There's no dial tone.
                  There's static on the line.
                  My phone is dead.
                  The outlet doesn't work.

INTERVIEW

1. Do you have a telephone?
2. Do you rent or own it?
3. Have you ever had a problem with your telephone?
   What did you do?
   Who had to pay to repair it?
4. What should you do if your phone doesn't work?

2

FOOD AND MONEY

COMPETENCY OBJECTIVES

On completion of this chapter the students will show orally, in writing, or through demonstration that they are able to use language needed in the following situations:

A. SHOPPING FOR FOOD

- Discuss the principles of comparison shopping, differentiating between various types of food stores.
- Identify quantities of food and how they are packaged and sold.
- Define and use the common U.S. weights and measures.
- Explain food classifications and ask for information regarding the location of food items.
- State dissatisfaction with an item purchased and express the need to return or exchange it.
- Read and interpret a grocery store ad.

B. MONEY AND CHANGE

- Make or respond to a request for change.
- Request the correct change when the incorrect change is given.

C. EATING OUT

- Place an order in a restaurant.
- Explain and calculate a tip.

D. PREPARING FOOD

- Describe how something is cooked.
- Read and interpret a food label.
- Read and interpret a recipe.

NEEDS ASSESSMENT EXERCISE _____

FOOD AND MONEY

I need to improve my English so that I can

_____ compare prices and find the best buys in food stores.

_____ understand how food is packaged and sold in the U.S.

_____ understand and use U.S. weights and measures.

_____ ask for information about where to find items in a food store.

_____ know how to complain about, exchange, or return something I bought in a food store.

_____ read and understand a grocery store or supermarket ad.

_____ ask for or respond to a request for change.

_____ order and pay for food in a restaurant.

_____ understand and figure the amount of a tip.

_____ tell someone how a particular kind of food is cooked.

_____ read and follow directions for recipes.

_____ read and understand labels on bottles, cans, and packages of food.

WHICH STORE IS BEST?

A: Oh, no! I'm out of sugar, and the supermarket is closed.
B: How much sugar do you need?
A: The recipe calls for 1 cup, and I only have 1/4 cup.
B: Should I run to the 7-Eleven? I can get the food for tomorrow's dinner at the same time.
A: Oh, no. Just get the sugar—we can wait for the other things. Food is too expensive there.

PRACTICE

Should I run to the 7-Eleven store?
      supermarket?
      fish market?
      grocery store?
      bakery?
      delicatessen/deli?

I only have 1/4 cup.
    1/2 cup.
    1/3 cup.

I'm out of sugar.
We're flour.
    salt.
    oil.
    shortening.
    pepper.
    baking soda.
    butter.

What do you need?
  are you out of?

INTERVIEW

1. Do you ever run out of any foods? Which ones?
2. Where do you usually go shopping for food? Why do you go to that store?

Pair Practice: Sit in pairs and ask each other the following kinds of questions about each item on the chart.

SAMPLE QUESTIONS

1. How much is a pound of chicken at _____ ?
2. Which store has the cheapest chicken?
3. Which store has the most expensive chicken?

EXAMPLE: Student A: How much is a pound of chicken at Store 1?
Student B: A pound of chicken at Store 1 costs 65 cents.

FOOD PRICES

	Store 1	Store 2	Store 3	Store 4
Whole chicken (1 lb.)	.65	.69	.75	.59
Bananas (lb.)	.39	.50	.39	.33
Lettuce (ea. head)	.59	.79	.59	.59
Apple juice (bottle)	1.71	1.89	1.79	1.37
Tide detergent (box)	2.39	2.24	2.64	2.14
Lowfat milk (gal.)	2.03	2.09	2.11	2.01

Take-Home Assignment:

1. Go to two or three grocery stores near your home and find the prices of the items on the chart below.
2. Write the information on the chart.
3. Share the information with students in your class, and compare the prices.

	Store:	Store:	Store:
Chicken (1 lb.)			
Oranges (1 lb.)			
Rice (5-lb. bag)			
Milk (1/2 gal.)			

BUYING FISH

A: Where can I buy some good fish?
B: Fed-Mart has the cheapest fish, but the fish at the fish market is fresher.
A: Is it more expensive, too?
B: Yes, but it tastes better. It's worth the difference.

PRACTICE

Fed-Mart has cheaper tomatoes than Food Basket.
        bigger
        juicier
        better

Fed-Mart has the cheapest fish.
        freshest
        nicest
        best

Food Basket has more expensive tomatoes than Save-Mart.
        delicious

The fish market has the most expensive fish.
        delicious

Pair Practice: Sit in pairs and ask each other the following questions.

Which store do you think has the cheapest meat?
        the best meat?
        the freshest vegetables?
        the most expensive fruit?
        the cheapest rice?
        the best rice?
        the fastest service?
        the slowest service?
        the best fruit?
        the best overall prices?

Pair Practice: Sit in pairs and role-play the following conversation using your own words.

A: Where can I buy/get some good _____ ?

B: _____ has the cheapest _____ ,

but the _____ at _____

is _____ .

GOING FOOD SHOPPING

A: I'm going to the store. Is there anything you need?

B: Yes, I need a few things. Would you please see if there's any milk in the refrigerator?

A: There's a little—about half a quart.

B: Is there any rice in the cupboard?

A: There's only about a cup. Should I get some?

B: Yes. What about eggs?

A: There are plenty of eggs—at least two dozen.

B: How about butter?

A: There isn't much left—just one stick.

B: Are there any green onions left?

A: No, they're all gone.

B: All right. Please get two bunches of green onions, a pound of butter, a package of rice, a gallon of milk, and a pint of ice cream.

SOME—ANY

I have *some* apples.
I don't have *any* apples.
Do you have *any* apples?

FEW—MANY

I have a *few* apples.
I don't have *many* apples.

LITTLE—MUCH

I have a *little* milk.
I don't have *much* milk.
How *much* milk do you have?

PRACTICE

I need a few things.
    apples.
    potatoes.
    onions.
    cans of tomato sauce.
    boxes of cereal.

There are plenty of eggs.
    a lot of
    many
    a couple of
    some

There's a little milk—about half a quart.
    butter   stick./cube.
    bread   loaf.
    ice cream pint.
    flour   cup.
    catsup   bottle.

There isn't much butter left.
    milk
    cheese
    garlic
    oil
    vinegar
    tea

Are there many green onions left?
    hot dogs
    napkins
    cookies
    bananas
    oranges

Please get two bunches of onions.
                carrots.
    heads of   lettuce.
                cabbage.
    loaves of bread.
    sticks of butter.
            margarine.

Box _____

With your class, make a list of the different ways we buy things—for example, in a box or can, or by the bunch or stick. Then think of different things we buy each way.

Pair Practice: Practice the following conversation with a partner.

A: What do you buy in a _____ or by the _____ ?

B: I buy _____ .

  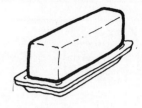

Pair Practice: Practice the conversations below with your class and then with a partner. Student A asks questions using *how much* or *how many*. Student B answers using the correct measurement words. Then Student B asks the questions, and Student A answers. Add questions about other things you buy at the market if you wish.

EXAMPLE 1. Student A: How many apples should I get?
               Student B: Get 2 pounds of apples, please.
            2. Student A: How much milk should I get?
               Student B: Get 1 gallon, please.

Student A	Student B
1. apples	1. 2 _____
2. milk	2. 1 _____
3. rice	3. 5 _____
4. eggs	4. 2 _____
5. cola	5. 2 _____
6. ice cream	6. 1 _____
7. butter	7. 2 _____
8. fish	8. 3 _____
9. _____	9. ? _____

Pair Practice: Practice the following conversation with your class, and then practice with a partner.

A: I'm going to the store. Is there anything you need?
B: Yes, I need a few things. Would you please see if there is
    any _____ ?
A: There is/are about _____ left.
B: Is/are there any _____ in the cupboard?
A: There _____ . Shall I get some?
B: Yes, what about _____ ?
A: There _____ .
B: Are there many _____ left?
A: There _____ .
B: All right. Get _____ .

FOOD CATEGORIES AND LOCATIONS

A: Excuse me, where can I find the eggs?
B: Go down aisle 3 and look in the dairy section. (Later) Did you find the eggs?
A: Yes, but now I can't find any fresh peaches. I looked in the produce section.
B: We're all out of peaches. We'll be getting more on Friday.

PRACTICE

Where can I find the rice?
        carrots?
        cookies?
        paper towels?
        mayonnaise?
        frozen orange juice?

Look in the cereal section.
        produce
        bakery
        paper goods
        canned goods
        frozen foods

Can you tell me where I can find fresh corn?
        canned
        frozen

We don't have any pork chops today.
        lamb
        chuck roast
        ground round
        stew meat

SOUR MILK

A: Is this the milk you bought at the store today?
B: Yes. Why?
A: It tastes sour.
B: Look at the expiration date on the top of the carton. What does it say?
A: It says, *Sell by May 13.*
B: Oh, no. I didn't look at the date. Now I'll have to make another trip to the store to return it.
A: Good luck.

RETURNING FOOD ITEMS

A: May I speak to the manager, please?
B: I'm the manager. What can I do for you?
A: I bought this milk here this morning. It tastes sour. The date says May 13, and today is May 15. Here, smell it.
B: Do you have your receipt?
A: Yes. Here it is, and here's the price of the milk. I underlined it.
B: Yes. I see. Usually our delivery man removes the older milk from the case before the expiration date. He must have missed this one. I'll replace it for you. Just a minute.
A: Thank you.

PRACTICE

May I speak to the manager, please?
      talk to
      see

Is the manager in?
I'd like to speak to the manager, please.
I want to speak to the manager, please.

It tastes sour.
      rotten.
      bitter.
      bad.

He must have missed this one.
      overlooked
      forgotten

INTERVIEW

1. Did you ever buy food that was spoiled? What kind of food was it?
2. What did you do? What did you say?
3. What did the clerk or manager do? What did the manager say?
4. What can you do if the manager doesn't agree with you?

The fish has worms in it.
The bread is moldy.
The flour has bugs in it.
The bread is stale.

Pair Practice: Sit in pairs and practice the conversation below. Substitute the listed words for the underlined words in the conversation.

A: May I speak to the manager?
B: I'm the manager.
    What's the problem?
A: I bought this <u>meat</u> here this morning.
    <u>It smells bad.</u>
B: Do you have your receipt?
A: Yes, here it is.

1. fish—worms
2. flour—bugs
3. pork—smells rotten

Pair Practice: Practice the dialogue again using only the cue words below.

A: May _____ manager?

B: I'm _____ .

    What's _____ ?

A: I bought _____ .

    It's _____ .

B: Do _____ receipt?

A: Yes. _____ .

INTERVIEW

1. What's happening in the picture?

   What's the customer at the checkout counter doing?
   What's the man beside the cashier doing?
   What's the man on the far left doing?
   Describe the people in the picture.

2. Where do you go grocery shopping?
3. Why do you go there?
4. How often do you go shopping?
5. Who does the food shopping in your house?
6. How often did you go food shopping in your country?
7. Are the food stores in the U.S. the same as those in your country?
8. How are they different?
9. What do you like about the food stores in the U.S.?
10. What don't you like about the food stores in the U.S.?
11. If you could change the food stores in the U.S., what would you do to make them better?

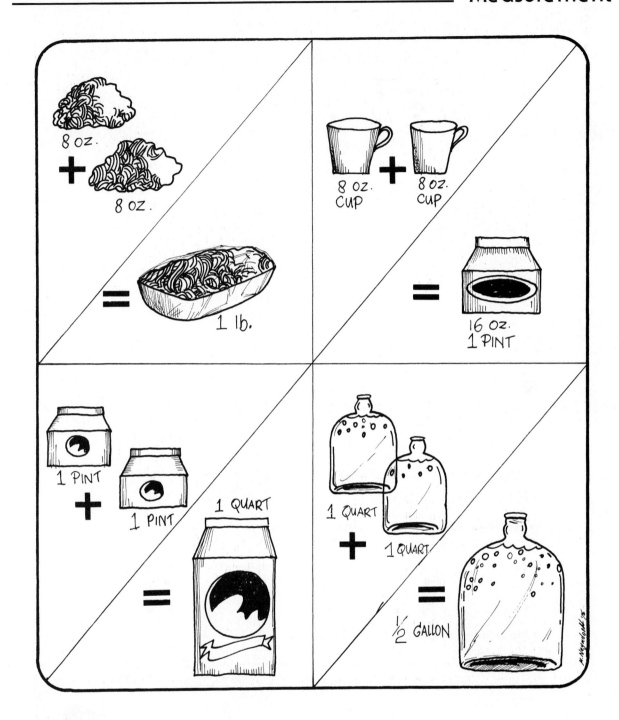

INTERVIEW

1. How many ounces are there in 1 pound?
2. How many ounces are there in 2 cups?
3. How many cups are there in 1 quart?
4. How many pints are there in 1/2 gallon?
5. How many quarts are there in 1 gallon?

SHARING RECIPES

A: This beef is delicious. How did you fix it?
B: It's easy. I just marinated it overnight and then broiled it.
A: Can you give me the recipe?
B: Sure. I'll bring it tomorrow.

PRACTICE

This beef is delicious.
    fish
    salad
    dessert
    dip
    sauce
    casserole
    soup

How did you fix it?
    prepare
    cook
    make

I just marinated it.
    broiled
    boiled
    fried
    steamed
    baked
    roasted
    barbecued

INTERVIEW

1. Do you like to cook?

   What do you like to cook?
   How do you cook it?

2. What is a popular dish in your country?
3. Do you know how to make it?

   (If yes) What do I need to make it?
   What do I do first?
   Then what do I do?
   How long does it take to make it?

LEMON PUDDING CAKE

1 pkg. lemon cake mix
1 pkg. (4 serving size) lemon instant pudding mix
½ cup oil; 1 cup water; 4 eggs

Blend ingredients on low speed until moistened (½ minute). Beat 2 minutes on medium speed. Bake in greased and floured pan in preheated 350°F oven. Cake is done when toothpick inserted in center comes out clean.

two 8" × 1½" round layers . . . . 30-35 minutes
two 9" × 1½" round layers . . . . 30-35 minutes
one 13" × 9½" × 2" oblong . . . . 37-42 minutes
one 10" fluted or tube . . . . 55-60 minutes

Cool in pan 15 minutes, remove, and cool topside up on cooling rack. Frost when cool, if desired.

Study the recipe above to answer the following questions:

1. How long should you bake two round cakes?

   a. 30–35 minutes
   b. 37–42 minutes
   c. 55–60 minutes
   d. 15–20 minutes

2. What should you do first?

   a. Blend the ingredients.
   b. Beat the ingredients.
   c. Frost the layers.
   d. Bake the cake.

3. How much water do you need to make the cake?

   a. ½ cup
   b. 1 cup
   c. 2 cups
   d. 5 teaspoons

4. How long should you beat the ingredients?

   a. ½ minute
   b. 2 minutes
   c. 15 minutes
   d. 1 minute

Study the supermarket ad above to answer the following questions:

1. How much do apples cost?

   a. 69¢ each
   b. $1.29 each
   c. 69¢ a pound
   d. $1.29 a pound

2. Which of the following sentences is true?

   a. Chicken is cheaper than ground beef.
   b. Ground beef is cheaper than chicken.
   c. Pears are more expensive than apples.
   d. Avocados are cheaper than lettuce.

3. What is the cheapest fruit advertised in the ad?

   a. pears
   b. strawberries
   c. apples
   d. oranges

UNDERSTANDING FOOD PRODUCT LABELS

The United States government has a law requiring that labels on all food products must list the ingredients in that product. The ingredients must be listed in order of quantity. The ingredient that is listed first is found in the greatest amount in that product.

INGREDIENTS: BEEF STOCK, CARROTS, POTATOES, TOMATOES, COOKED BEEF, WATER, CELERY, BURGUNDY WINE, CORN STARCH, NATURAL FLAVORINGS

VEGETABLE & BEEF SOUP

Study the label above to answer the following questions:

1. Which ingredient is there the most of?
2. Is there more beef stock than wine in the soup?
3. Are there more potatoes than tomatoes in the soup?
4. Is there more cooked beef than potatoes in the soup?
5. Are there more carrots than beef?
6. Which ingredient is there the least of?
7. If you made this soup, would you add any other ingredients?
8. Would you take out any ingredients?
9. Do you think you would like this soup?
10. What kind of soup do you like best? What ingredients do you need to make it?

ASKING FOR CHANGE

A: Excuse me, do you have change for a dollar?
   I need the exact change
   for the soft drink machine.
B: Just a minute. Let me check.
A: I usually have a lot of change, but
   today I only have a few pennies.
B: I only have 50¢ in change. Maybe
   you can get some change at the corner market.
A: Thanks, I'll try.
B: I'm sorry I couldn't help you.

PRACTICE

Do you have change for a dollar?
                        five?
                        twenty?
                        quarter?

I only have a few cents.
              dimes.
              quarters.
              dollars.

Pair Practice: Sit in pairs and practice the conversation below. Use your own words to fill in the blanks.

A: Excuse me, do you have change for _____ ?

   I need the exact change for _____ .

B: Just a minute. Let me check.

A: I usually have _____ , but today I only have

   _____ .

B: I only have _____ . Maybe you can get some

   _____ at the _____ .

A: Thank you.

WRONG CHANGE

A: That comes to $6.45, please.
B: Here you are.
A: Thank you. Here's your change. That was six forty-five, fifty, seven, eight, nine, and ten.
B: Excuse me. I think you made a mistake. I gave you a twenty-dollar bill, and you only gave me change for a ten.
A: Just a minute. Let me check the cash drawer. Oh, you're right. Here it is, right on top. I'm sorry. That was six forty-five, seven, eight, nine, ten and ten is twenty.
B: Thank you.

PRACTICE

Excuse me, I gave you a twenty dollar bill.
                        ten
                        five
                        hundred
You only gave me change for a ten.
                         five.
                         twenty.
Excuse me. I think you gave me the wrong change.
                   made a mistake.

INTERVIEW

1. Did you ever get the wrong change?
2. When did it happen?
3. Where did it happen?
4. What did you do?
5. If you got the wrong change and the cashier refused to correct the mistake, what could you do?
   What would you say to the cashier?

EATING OUT

A:	Could we have a table for four, please?
Waitress:	There will be a 15-minute wait.
A:	That's OK. May we look over the menu before we sit down?
Waitress:	(Later) Right this way. Your table is ready now. (Hands them menus after they are seated)
Waitress:	(Later) Are you ready to order now?
A:	Yes, please. I think I'll have the steak and shrimp combination.
Waitress:	How would you like your steak?
A:	Medium rare, please.
Waitress:	Would you like soup or salad?
A:	Does it come with the meal?
Waitress:	Yes, it does.
A:	I'd like a salad, please, with Thousand Island dressing.
Waitress:	Would you like a baked potato, french fries, or rice?
A:	A baked potato, please, with sour cream.
Waitress:	Will there be anything else?
A:	No, thank you. That will be all.
Waitress:	And you, sir?

PRACTICE

How would you like your steak?

I'd like it rare, please.
          medium rare.
          medium well.
          well done.

I'll have salad, please, with Thousand Island dressing.
          Roquefort dressing.
          French dressing.
          oil and vinegar.
          Italian dressing.

DINNER MENU

Appetizers: Shrimp cocktail 3.95
Assorted hors d'oeuvres 3.95
French onion soup 2.95
Clam chowder 2.25

A La Carte: Spaghetti 4.50
Fried chicken 5.25
Broiled fish 6.00
Ham with pineapple 4.75
Cheeseburger 3.25

Dinners: The dinners are served with soup or salad, your choice of dressing—blue cheese, Thousand Island, or French, baked or french-fried potatoes, and bread and butter.

Fried chicken 6.90
Golden fried shrimp 7.95
Top sirloin steak 9.45
Roast turkey dinner 6.50
Broiled fish 7.50

Child's Plate: Hamburger patty, fried potatoes, and milk 2.95

Side Orders: Baked potato 1.00
Onion rings 1.50
Chef's salad bowl 3.00
Corn on the cob (in season) 1.25

Desserts: Pie 1.50
Cake 1.50
Pudding, vanilla or chocolate 1.00
Ice cream or sherbert 1.00
Hot fudge sundae 1.95
Strawberry shortcake 2.00

Beverages: Coffee .... .50
Tea .... .50
Milk .... .55
Coca Cola .... .50   large .... .70
7-Up .... .50   large .... .70
Beer 1.00
Iced Tea .... .60

Pair Practice: Sit in pairs and role-play the conversation below, using the menu on page 45.

A: = waiter or waitress
B: = customer

A: Are you ready to order?
B: (Order from the menu.)
A: How would you like your meat?
B: (Answer.)
A: Would you like soup or salad?
B: (Ask if it comes with the meal.)
A: (Answer.)
   Will there be anything else?
B: (Ask for the check with the meal.)

Task Assignment: If possible, get a menu from a restaurant in your area or make up a fast food menu. Then role-play the dialogue above, using the new menu.

INTERVIEW

1. Do you ever go to restaurants? Why? Why not?
2. What restaurant did you go to last?
   Who did you go with?
   What did you order?
   Did you enjoy what you ordered?
3. Do you like to go out to eat?
4. What is your favorite kind of restaurant food?
5. If you could go to to any restaurant, which one would you go to? Why?

15% TIP TABLE			
Check	Tip	Check	Tip
$1.00	$.15	$26.00	$3.90
2.00	.30	27.00	4.05
3.00	.45	28.00	4.20
4.00	.60	29.00	4.35
5.00	.75	30.00	4.50
6.00	.90	31.00	4.65
7.00	1.05	32.00	4.80
8.00	1.20	33.00	4.95
9.00	1.35	34.00	5.10
10.00	1.50	35.00	5.25
11.00	1.65	36.00	5.40
12.00	1.80	37.00	5.55
13.00	1.95	38.00	5.70
14.00	2.10	39.00	5.85
15.00	2.25	40.00	6.00
16.00	2.40	41.00	6.15
17.00	2.55	42.00	6.30
18.00	2.70	43.00	6.45
19.00	2.85	44.00	6.60
20.00	3.00	45.00	6.75
21.00	3.15	46.00	6.90
22.00	3.30	47.00	7.05
23.00	3.45	48.00	7.20
24.00	3.60	49.00	7.35
25.00	3.75	50.00	7.50

TIP

A: May we have the check, please?
B: Certainly. Here it is.
A: It's less than I expected.
C: Don't forget the tip. How much does the bill come to?
A: The total is $5.00. How much should we leave?
C: We should leave 15% or 20% of the total price.
A: Let's see. How about 75¢. Just a minute—I'll have to get some change from the cashier.

PRACTICE

It's less than I expected.
    cheaper
    bigger
    more expensive
How much should I leave?
              pay?
I'll have to get some change.
              quarters.
              dimes.
I'll have to leave a tip.
       charge it.
       put it on my credit card.
       borrow some money.

INTERVIEW

Did you leave a tip in restaurants in your country?
How much?

chapter 3

HEALTH CARE

COMPETENCY OBJECTIVES

On completion of this unit the students will show orally, in writing, or through demonstration that they are able to use language needed in the following situations:

A. MEDICAL PROBLEMS

- Identify external and internal parts of the body.
- Describe health problems or injuries in detail, stating symptoms, the frequency of symptoms, and/or possible causes.
- Report results of a visit to a doctor, clinic, or hospital.

B. MEDICAL APPOINTMENTS/MEDICAL HISTORY

- Use the telephone to make a medical or dental appointment.
- Describe general medical history, including previous illnesses, injuries, and operations.
- Fill out a medical history form with assistance.
- Read and interpret an immunization record.

C. MEDICINE/PRESCRIPTIONS

- Follow oral or written instructions related to medications and treatment.
- Request a prescription or a prescription refill at a drug store or pharmacy.
- Read and interpret medicine labels.

D. EMERGENCIES/SAFETY

- Respond effectively to health emergencies by calling the police, paramedics, poison information center, and/or hospital.
- Recognize and correct potential dangers in the home.
- Read and interpret information from a poison information center.

NEEDS ASSESSMENT EXERCISE _____

HEALTH CARE

I need to improve my English so that I can

_____ identify the external and internal parts of my body.

_____ describe medical problems or injuries to a doctor or nurse.

_____ report results of a visit to a doctor, clinic, or hospital.

_____ make a medical or dental appointment on the telephone.

_____ describe my medical history, including previous illnesses, injuries, and operations.

_____ fill out a medical history form for myself or my child.

_____ read and understand an immunization record.

_____ follow instructions for taking medicine.

_____ follow instructions for taking care of myself or my children after an illness or injury.

_____ request a prescription or a prescription refill at a drug store or pharmacy.

_____ read and understand labels on medicines.

_____ get help in emergencies by calling the police, paramedics, poison center, or hospital.

_____ recognize possible unsafe conditions or dangers in my home and get help taking care of them.

A: My son <u>Tom</u> won't be at school today.
B: What seems to be the trouble?
A: He has a rash. I think he's coming down with the measles.
   He's been exposed to them.
B: What grade is he in?
A: Third grade.
B: Who's his teacher?
A: Mr. Brown.
B: OK. Thanks for calling. I'll let his teacher know.

PRACTICE

I think he's coming down with the measles.
                              the flu.
                              a cold.

He's been exposed to the measles.
                      mumps.
                      chicken pox.

Pair Practice: Practice the dialogue below with your class and then in pairs. Substitute the listed words for the underlined words in the dialogue.

(sore throat—flu)
Example: Student A: My son won't be at school today.
              Student B: What seems to be the trouble?

              Student A: He has <u>a sore throat.</u> I think he's coming down with
              <u>the flu</u> .

   1. swollen glands—mumps
   2. runny nose—cold
   3. stomachache—flu
   4. earache—ear infection

Small Group Practice: Sit in groups of four. Student 1 asks a question. Student 2 answers the question and asks student 3 a question. Student 3 answers the question and asks student 4 a question, and so on. Try to ask the question in a different way each time.

Example: Student A: What's the matter?
                               or
              What's wrong?

              Student B: I have a _____ .
                               or

              My _____ hurts.
                    or

              I think I am coming down with _____ .

Pair Practice: Sit in pairs and ask each other questions using the information on the chart.

	Measles	When	Chicken Pox	When
John	Yes	7 years old	Yes	9 years old
Ann	No		Yes	14 years old
Lee	Yes	20 years ago	Yes	15 years ago
You				

EXAMPLE: Student A: Has John ever had the measles?
               Student B: Yes, he has.
               Student A: When?
               Student B: When he was seven years old.

Pair Practice: Practice the conversation below with your teacher. Then practice with a partner. Substitute the listed words for the underlined words in the dialogue.

EXAMPLE: Student A: (Asks the question) Have you ever had <u>the chicken pox</u> ?
               Student B: (Answers the question and then adds another statement)
                              Yes. I had them when I was a child.
               Student A: (Responds to what student B said) Really? I have never had them.

1. chicken pox
2. measles
3. mumps
4. polio
5. tuberculosis
6. an operation
7. high blood pressure
8. allergies
9. kidney trouble
10. bad headaches

INTERVIEW

1. Do you have children?
2. Have any of your children ever had the chicken pox, mumps, or measles?
3. If yes, when did they have them?
4. In your country, did children get the same diseases?
5. In your country, what diseases did you worry about?
6. Do children get vaccinated in your country?

Keeping Immunization Records

FAMILY IMMUNIZATION RECORD Ask your doctor about these. When shots are given, keep a record.	
Shots for Diphtheria, Tetanus, Whooping Cough One vaccine (one shot each date) can immunize for all three if doctor recommends.	At age 2 months
	2 months later
	2 months later
	12 months later
	Booster 4–6 years old
Polio One oral vaccine each date.	At age 2 months
	2 months later
	2 months later
	12 months later
	Booster 4–6 years old
Measles, Mumps, Rubella Triple vaccination shot for all three diseases if doctor recommends. No boosters.	After 1 year old
	After 1 year old
	After 1 year old

Study the family immunization record above to answer the following questions.

1. What shots should a two-month old baby get?

   a. polio and measles only
   b. polio, diptheria, tetanus, and whooping cough
   c. polio, measles, mumps, and tetanus
   d. only diptheria, tetanus, and whooping cough

2. How many polio vaccines does a child need before he or she is two years old?

   a. 2
   b. 3
   c. 4
   d. 5

3. If a child gets a polio vaccine at two months old, when should he or she get the next one?

   a. at 4 months old
   b. at 6 months old
   c. at 1 year old
   d. at 4 years old

DESCRIBING SYMPTOMS

A: What seems to be the problem?
B: My stomach is bothering me.
A: Can you describe your symptoms?
B: It feels like it is on fire.
A: How long have you had this problem?
B: On and off for about a month.
A: When does it hurt?
B: It usually hurts before I eat. Sometimes I feel better after I eat.
A: Are you taking any medication for it now?
B: No.
A: OK. Try taking a tablespoon of this before each meal. If it doesn't help, please come back to see me, and we'll run some tests.

PRACTICE

What seems to be the problem?
                    bothering you?

What's the matter?
        wrong?

My stomach is bothering me.
    back
    knee
    shoulder

It hurts before I eat.
        when I walk.
        when I worry.
        when I run.
        when I bend over.
        after I eat.
        after I exercise.

How long have you had this problem?
Since Friday.
        last month.
        last week.
        1983.

We'll run some tests.
        take some tests.
        take some X rays.

Can you describe the symptoms?

It feels like it is on fire.
            hot.
            numb.
            cold.

It throbs.
    itches.
    aches.
    tingles.

For five days.
    one week.
    two months.
    a few hours.

Pair Practice: Look at the pictures and ask questions with *How long*. Use *since* or *for* in your answers.

EXAMPLE: Student A: How long has she had a headache?
Student B: She has had a headache for several hours.

PRACTICE WITH *SINCE* AND *FOR*

Use *since* or *for* in each blank space.

1.   I have been sick _____ Friday.

2.   She has had a headache _____ three days.

3.   I have had a stomachache _____ one week.

4.   I haven't had the flu _____ last year.

5.   My children haven't been to a doctor _____ last September.

6.   He has had problems with his back _____ a long time.

7.   We have had the same doctor _____ 1960.

8.   She has had a swollen ankle _____ she fell down the stairs last Friday.

9.   How long has it been _____ you had a tetanus shot?

10. He has had an eye infection _____ several days.

A: I can't come to school for a few weeks.
B: Oh, why not?
A: I'm going to have an operation.
B: What kind?
A: I'm going to have eye surgery.
B: I hope it's nothing serious.
A: Oh, no. The doctor says I should be OK after a few weeks.
B: That's good.

PRACTICE

I'm going to have eye surgery.
    heart
    hip
    knee

I'm going to have a tumor removed.
    growth
    cataract
    mole

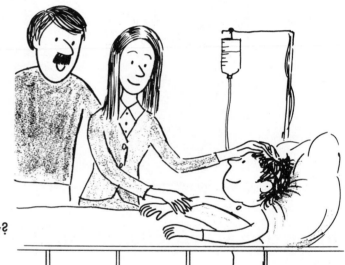

INTERVIEW

1. Have you ever had surgery?
   Where?
   When?
   Why?
   How long did you stay in the hospital?
2. Do you know anyone else
   who has had an operation?
   Tell me about it.
3. How are hospitals in your country
   the same as or different from hospitals in the U.S.?
4. What do you like about medical care in the U.S.?
5. What don't you like about medical care here?

INSIDE THE BODY

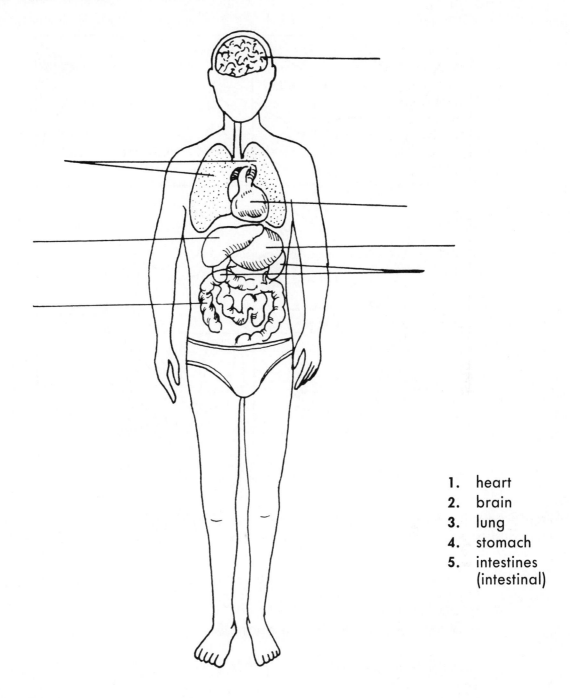

1. heart
2. brain
3. lung
4. stomach
5. intestines
   (intestinal)

PRACTICE

Write the number of each internal organ listed above on the correct line. Then practice the dialogue below with your class and then with a partner, substituting items 1 – 5 in the blank space.

A: Tom won't be at work for a few weeks.
B: Why not?

A: He's going to have _____ surgery.

Pair Practice: Practice the following conversation with your class and then with a partner. Substitute the information listed below for the underlined words in the dialogue.

EXAMPLE: Student A: Oh, what happened?

Student B: I hurt my _wrist_ .
Student A: How did you do that?

Student B: I _sprained_ it while I was _fixing the fence_ .

1. finger
   burned it
   cooking

2. ankle
   twisted it
   walking downstairs

3. arm
   broke it
   painting the ceiling

4. thumb
   cut it
   chopping onions

5. back
   strained it
   picking up a box

6. elbow
   scraped it
   playing tennis

DOCTOR'S APPOINTMENT

A: Mid-City Clinic.
B: This is Anne Lee. I would like to make an appointment to see Dr. Jones.
A: Certainly. How about next Tuesday? Can you come in then?
B: Could I come in sooner than that? I have a pain in my stomach, and I feel terrible.
A: Let me check the book. I think I could fit you in today at 2:30, but you might have to wait a little bit.
B: That's all right. I don't mind waiting.
A: We'll see you about 2:30 then. Please call if you can't keep the appointment.

PRACTICE

I'd like to make an appointment to see Dr. Jones.
       cancel my
       postpone
       change
       put off

I don't mind waiting.
       standing.
       taking medicine.
       getting an X ray.

Could I come in sooner than that?
       later
       earlier

You might have to wait a little bit.
       miss work.
       go into the hospital.
       have surgery.
       stay in bed.
       see another doctor.
       get an X ray.
       go on a diet.
       take an antibiotic.

INTERVIEW

1. Have you had an appointment with a doctor or dentist in the U.S.?
2. Did you speak English with the nurse or doctor?
3. When you went to the doctor, what did he or she ask you?
4. What did the doctor do?
5. Did you have any problems talking with the doctor or understanding the doctor?

AT THE DOCTOR'S OFFICE

Patient: Good morning. I'm Juan Carillo.
I have an appointment with the doctor at 11:00.
Nurse: Are you coming in for a flu shot?
Patient: No, I've already been vaccinated at the public health department.
I want the doctor to look at my leg. It's swollen.
Nurse: All right, please fill out this health form first.
The examination will be $40.00.
Patient: I think my health insurance will cover this office visit.
Here's my card.
Nurse: Thank you. Please have a seat until we call you.

PRACTICE

Does your health insurance plan cover hospitalization?
office visits?
dental care?
prescriptions?
X rays?
laboratory work?

I want him to look at my swollen leg.
you   rash.
her   bruised arm.
them   cut finger.
sprained ankle.

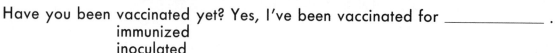

Have you ever had a broken leg?
sprained ankle?
serious illness?
an operation?
X ray?

I've already been vaccinated.
inoculated.
X-rayed.
examined.
operated on.

Have you been vaccinated yet? Yes, I've been vaccinated for _____ .
immunized
inoculated

INTERVIEW

1. What diseases are people immunized for in your country?
2. Have you or your children been immunized for any diseases in the United States? Which diseases?

STANDARD HEALTH EXAMINATION RECORD

Date ___/___/___   Name _____   Age _____ Sex _____
   mo day year   (last)   (first)
   Address _____ Phone _____ Birthdate _____

MEDICAL HISTORY

HAVE YOU HAD ANY PROBLEMS WITH:
   (check ✔)

PAST ILLNESSES	DISEASES	IMMUNIZATIONS-TESTS
Frequent colds _____	Chicken pox _____	Diphtheria _____
Frequent sore throats _____	Measles _____	Whooping Cough _____
Bronchitis _____	Mumps _____	Poliomyelitis _____
Allergies _____	Scarlet Fever _____	Tetanus _____
Operations or serious	Poliomyelitis _____	Smallpox _____
injuries _____	Whooping Cough _____	Typhoid _____
Stomach upsets _____	Other _____	Tuberculin _____
Kidney trouble _____		Other _____ _____
Convulsions _____		
Tuberculosis _____		List of Medications You Are Now Taking:
Diabetes _____		
Blood diseases (anemia, etc.) ___	SURGERIES DATE	_____
High blood pressure _____		
Heart attacks _____		
Mental depression _____	_____ ____	_____
Bad headaches or migraines ___		
Liver trouble (hepatitis) _____	_____ ____	_____
	_____ ____	
		Allergies to Medications:
	_____ ____	
		_____
	_____ ____	

ROLE PLAY

Talk about the illnesses, diseases and immunizations listed on the form with your teacher and class. Be sure you can read and say each one. Talk about what kind of illness or disease each one is. Then sit with a partner. One person is the doctor or nurse; the other is the patient. The doctor or nurse asks the questions and completes the form with information from the patient.

EXAMPLE:

Have you had any problem with _____ ?

Have you had _____ ?

Have you ever had _____ ?

Then fill in a copy of the form for yourself.

WHAT DID THE DOCTOR TELL YOU? _____

A: I'm sorry that I couldn't come to school yesterday.
B: Were you sick?
A: No, I had to go for a check-up.
B: Is everything OK?
A: Yes, except for my blood pressure. It's a little high.
B: What did the doctor tell you?
A: He told me to lose about 5 pounds and cut down on salt.
B: Did he take any other tests?
A: Yes, he took a chest X ray, and it was OK.
B: That's good.

PRACTICE

I couldn't come to school.
            work.
            the party.

He told me to lose 5 pounds.
              gain 5 pounds.
              cut down on salt.
              drink more water.
              cut down on fatty foods.
              get more exercise.
              eat more vegetables.

He told me not to eat junk food.
                 use so much salt.
                 drink too much.
                 smoke.
                 eat too many sweets.

He took a chest X ray.
            urine sample.
            blood test.
        my pulse.
        my blood pressure.

Small Group Practice: Practice the conversation below with your class. Then sit in groups of three and practice it again using the substitutions below.

EXAMPLE: Student A: (Doctor) You should *lose 5 pounds.*
                Student B: What did the doctor tell you?
                Student C: (Patient) He/She told me to *lose 5 pounds.*

1. Drink more water.
2. Get more exercise.
3. Stop smoking.
4. Cut down on salt.
5. Eat more fruit.
6. Get more sleep.
7. Eat more vegetables.
8. Take a nap every afternoon.
9. Come back in one week.
10. Take the medicine until it is gone.

NO SMOKING

Small Group Practice: Practice the conversation below with your class. Then sit in groups of three and practice it again substituting items 1–10.

EXAMPLE: Student A (the doctor):   Don't eat sugar.
                Student B (a friend):   What did the doctor tell you?
                Student C (the patient):   He/She told me not to eat sugar.

1. Don't work too hard.
2. Don't drink alcoholic beverages.
3. Don't worry.
4. Don't eat a lot of salt.
5. Don't smoke.
6. Don't eat a lot of starchy food.
7. Don't gain any more weight.
8. Don't eat a lot of junk food.
9. Don't stay up too late at night.
10. Don't be late for your appointment.

PRESCRIPTION REFILL

A: Pharmacy. May I help you?
B: Yes. I've run out of my antibiotic. I need a refill.
A: Sorry, but your prescription was only for one bottle. You'll have to check with your doctor.
B: Do I have to go back to the doctor again?
A: No, you can ask him or her to call us.
B: OK. I'll try that. By the way, could you please give me the generic brand this time?
A: Sure.

PRACTICE

I've run out of this prescription.
     antibiotic.
     ointment.
     cream.
     cough syrup.
    these vitamins.
     drops.
     pills.

Do I have to go back to the doctor?
     sign the form?
     pay for it now?
     keep this in the refrigerator?
     take this until it is finished?

Could you give me the generic brand?
     a child-proof cap?
     a dropper?
     the directions?
     a receipt?

INTERVIEW

1. Have you ever gotten a prescription filled in the U.S.?

   For what problem?
   Where did you get it filled?
   Did you get a refill?
   Did the medicine make you feel better?
   Did you finish the medicine?
   Would you have been treated differently for this illness in your country?

2. Have you ever had any problems with taking American medicine?

3. What kind of medicine did you use in your country? Did you need a prescription?

UNDERSTANDING MEDICINE LABELS

Study the medicine labels on page 66 to decide if the following statements are true or false.

EXAMPLE:

Label 1

__T__ You should close lids tightly.

Label 1

_____ You should always save old medicines.

Label 2

_____ An adult can take 2 teaspoons of the cough syrup.

_____ A child 10 years old can take no more than 1/2 teaspoon of the cough syrup.

Label 3

_____ An adult should take at least 8 B-2 cold tablets a day.

Label 4

_____ If an adult is constipated, he or she should take 1 to 4 teaspoons of Flip's Milk of Magnesia.

_____ A child should not take Flip's Milk of Magnesia.

Label 5

_____ Children under 6 shouldn't use 1-Way nasal spray.

Label 6

_____ If you get a mosquito bite, you should use Deep Heat on it.

_____ Deep Heat will help a sunburn.

Label 7

_____ You can only use the eye drops twice a day.

1. **HOW TO USE MEDICINES**

Read and follow label instructions.
Keep lid tightly closed.
Shake before using.

Avoid excessive heat.
If symptoms persist, consult physician.
Dispose of old medicines properly.

2. **COUGH SYRUP**

Adults: 1 to 2 teaspoonfuls.

Children: 6-12 years—1/2 to 1 teaspoonful.
2-6 years—1/2 teaspoonful.

May be repeated in 4 hours, if necessary, but not more than 4 times in 24 hours.

For the relief of coughs due to colds. If cough lasts more than a week, consult your physician.

3. **B-2 COLD TABLETS**

Use: Relieves nasal congestion, running nose, watery eyes, and sneezing associated with common colds and hay fever.

Dosage: 2 tablets to start, followed by 1 tablet every 4 hours, not to exceed 8 tablets in 24 hours.

Children: 6–12—One-half adult dosage.

Continue treatment for 72 hours. This preparation may cause drowsiness. Do not drive or operate machinery while taking this medication.

4. FLIP'S MILK OF MAGNESIA

Adults: As an antacid—1 to 4 teaspoonfuls with a little water.

As a laxative—2 to 4 tablespoonfuls in a glass of water.

Children: 1/4 to 1/2 of adult dose.

5. **1-WAY NASAL SPRAY**

Adults: Spray once or twice in each nostril with head upright. Squeeze bottle quickly and firmly.

Children: Spray once.
Not recommended for children under 6.

The use of this dispenser by more than one person may spread infection.

6. **DEEP HEAT**

Penetrating pain relief.
Relieves muscular aches and pains.

Directions: Spread liberally over painful areas. Repeat every 4 hours if needed.

Warning: For external use only.

Discontinue use if skin rash or itching occurs.

7. **EYEDROPS**

For soothing and cleansing eyes.

Squeeze 2 or more drops into each eye as needed. Replace cap.

Do not touch dropper tip to any surface.

AT THE DENTIST'S OFFICE

A: How about going shopping today?
B: I'd like to, but I've got a dentist's appointment at 2:00.
A: What's wrong? Do you have a cavity that needs filling?
B: Oh, no. I'm just going in to have my teeth cleaned so that I don't get any cavities.
A: You're smart. I just had three teeth filled and one tooth pulled. My mouth was so sore I couldn't eat *anything*!
B: Or *buy* anything, either, I bet. Dental work isn't cheap.

PRACTICE

I've got a dentist's appointment.
        doctor's

Do you have a cavity that needs filling?
        tooth   pulling?
        filling   fixing?

I'm going to have my teeth cleaned.
                X-rayed.
                pulled.
                filled.

I just had three teeth filled.
              pulled.
              extracted.
              X-rayed.
              cleaned.

My mouth was so sore I couldn't eat.
        numb   talk.
        swollen   chew.
                close my mouth.

INTERVIEW

1. Have you had your teeth X-rayed in the U.S.? Where?
                        cleaned
                        examined
2. Do you like going to the dentist?
Why? Why not?
3. How is dental care in the U.S. different from dental care in your country?

EMERGENCY PHONE CALLS

DIAL 911

A: This is an emergency. I need a paramedic.
B: What's the matter?
A: I think my wife is having a heart attack.
B: What's your address?
A: 6231 Fir Street. Apartment 10.
B: What's the nearest cross street?
A: University Ave.
B: Please give me your name and the telephone number you are calling from.
A: 232-5631. My name is John Brown.
B: We'll send a paramedic immediately.

PRACTICE

This is an emergency! Give me the police!
                                   poison center!
                                   fire department!

I need an ambulance.
       a police officer.
       a doctor.

What do you think is wrong?
                   the matter?
                   the problem?
                   the emergency?

My father is having a heart attack.
                      stroke
                      chest pains.
              unconscious.
              bleeding.
         cut his hand.
         burned his arm.

INTERVIEW

1. Have you ever had to make an emergency telephone call?
2. What was the problem?
3. What happened?

Discuss each picture with your teacher and then with your class. What is happening? What could/might happen? What should the parents do to prevent such potential accidents? What should/could the parents do if an accident resulted?

EMERGENCY TELEPHONE NUMBERS

Write in the numbers for the city where you live.

1. Doctor _____

2. Emergency (crime in progress—life threatening) _____

3. Police (crime not in progress) _____

4. Fire Department _____

5. Poison Center _____

_____ FOLLOWING POISON CENTER RECOMMENDATIONS

POISON CENTER RECOMMENDATIONS

The Poison Center Council recommends several simple ways to protect your home from accidental poisonings:

> Install child-proof locks on all medicine cabinets and cupboards where dangerous substances are kept.
> Store cleaning materials in a locked cabinet which children can't open.
> Keep hazardous substances in their original containers. Never put them in a bottle or jar that once held food or drink.
> Label pill bottles, and never put different types of pills in the same bottle.
> Flush old medicines down the toilet.

Study the Poison Center recommendations above to decide if the following statements are true or false.

_____ 1. If you have small children, you should put locks on medicine cabinets.

_____ 2. You should store cleaning materials and medicines together in the same cabinet.

_____ 3. You should always save old medicines. Don't throw them away.

_____ 4. You should label all pill bottles.

_____ 5. You should not put medicine in jars that have had food in them.

In case of an accidental poisoning, the doctor or poison center will want to know:

What did you swallow?
        he drink?
        she ingest?
          eat?
          come in contact with?

How much did you swallow?
When did the poisoning occur?
        it happen?

What are your symptoms?
        the patient's symptoms?
        his
        her

How old is the patient?
        are you?

How much do you weigh?
        does he/she weigh?

In case of a poisoning, you should: Call your doctor or the poison center immediately! A glass of water or milk will help dilute the poison. Ipecac, an antidote for poisoning, will induce vomiting. You should keep it on hand. Your doctor or the poison center will tell you when to use it. There are times when you should *not* induce vomiting. Be sure to call the poison center or your doctor for information.

Look up the telephone number of your local Poison Control Center. Put it by your telephone. Practice what you would say if you called the Center.

chapter 4

TRANSPORTATION

COMPETENCY OBJECTIVES

On completion of this unit the students will show orally, in writing, or through demonstration that they are able to use language needed in the following situations:

A. DIRECTIONS

- Ask for, follow, and give directions to specific places.

B. TAKING THE BUS

- Ask for information regarding local and out-of-town bus schedules.
- Interpret a bus schedule.

C. MAINTAINING A CAR

- Describe common car problems.
- Identify basic parts of a car.
- Interpret instructions for using a gasoline pump.

D. DRIVING A CAR

- Describe a minor car accident.
- Answer a police officer's questions regarding a traffic violation.
- Interpret rules to follow in case of an accident.
- Read and complete a driver's license application.

E. PURCHASING A CAR

- Identify what to look for and ask questions in order to purchase a car.
- Interpret newspaper ads for new and used cars.
- Ask and answer questions related to automobile insurance.

NEEDS ASSESSMENT EXERCISE _____

TRANSPORTATION

I need to improve my English so that I can

_____ ask for and follow directions to places.

_____ give directions to places.

_____ ask for information about local and out-of-town bus transportation.

_____ read and understand a bus schedule.

_____ identify the parts of a car.

_____ describe problems with my car.

_____ get services and repairs for my car.

_____ answer a police officer's questions if I am stopped for a possible traffic violation.

_____ know what to do if I have an automobile accident.

_____ read and fill out an application for a driver's license.

_____ know what to look for and what questions to ask to purchase a car.

_____ read and understand newspaper ads for new and used cars.

_____ ask and answer questions about automobile insurance.

WHERE IS THE EMPLOYMENT OFFICE?

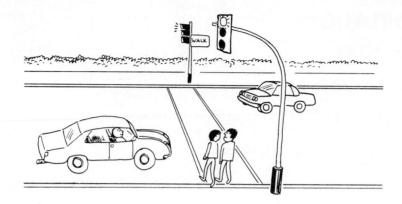

A: Excuse me, can you tell me how to get to the employment office?
B: Sure. It's not far.
   Walk straight ahead until you come to First Street.
A: What street?
B: First Street.
A: And about how many blocks is that?
B: About two blocks. Turn right on First Street. It's in the middle of
   the block.
A: Is it on the right or left side?
B: It's on the right side between the bank and the beauty shop. It's
   across the street from the parking lot.
A: Thanks a lot. I'm sure I can find it.
B: You can't miss it. It's easy to find.

PRACTICE

Can you tell me how to get to the employment office?
                              find the post office?
                    where to park?

It's in the middle of the block.
     at the end
     at the beginning

Walk straight ahead until you come to First Street.
     up the block
     down the street
     two blocks

It's on the right-hand side between the bank and the beauty shop.
                              next to the bank.
                              beside the bank.
                              across the street from the bank.
                              near the bank.

Turn left on First Street.
     right at the next intersection.
                    corner.
                    bank.
                    signal.

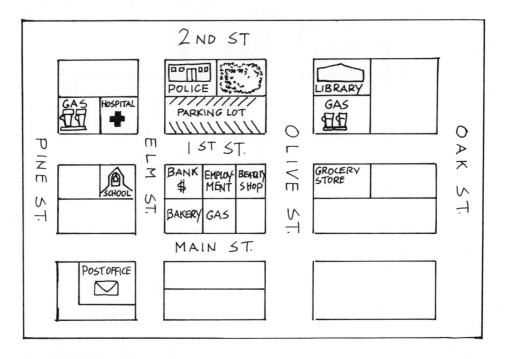

Pair Practice: Student A uses the map above to answer the questions below. Student B asks the questions.

1. Where is the school?
2. Where is the library?
3. How far is the bakery from the police station?

4. I am at _____ now. Can you tell me how to get to the hospital?
5. I am at school now. How do I get to the nearest gas station?

Practice Again: Student A asks the questions, and student B answers the questions. Practice writing the directions your partner gives you.

Student A: I'm at the school. How do I get to grocery store? (Write down the directions that student B gives you.)

Student B: I'm at the school. How do I get to the post office? (Write down the directions that student A gives you.)

INTERVIEW

1. Do you live far from school?
2. Where do you live?
3. Could you give me directions to your home from here?
4. How long does it take to get to your house?
5. Have you ever asked for directions? What happened?
6. If somebody gave you directions and you didn't understand, what would you say?

FREEWAY TO THE ZOO

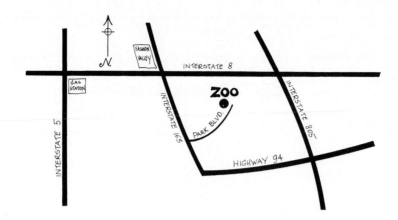

A: Excuse me, I'm lost. Can you help me?
B: I'll try. Where do you want to go?
A: I want to go to the zoo.
B: Follow this street past the next stoplight. You'll see the sign for Interstate 163 North. Go past that exit about a half mile. Take the turnoff for 163 south.
A: After I'm on the freeway, which exit should I take to get to the zoo?
B: Take the Park Boulevard exit and follow the signs.
A: That sounds simple to me.
B: Oh, you can't miss it. The signs are easy to follow.

PRACTICE

Where do you want to go?

I want to go to the zoo.   That sounds simple to me.
  plan   hard
  intend   easy
  hope   confusing

Pair Practice: Study the map above. Then answer the questions that your partner asks.

1. I'm at the gas station at Interstate 5 and 8.
   Please tell me how to get to the zoo.
2. Please tell me how to get to Fashion Valley from the gas station.
3. Which exit should I take off Interstate 8 to go to the zoo?
4. Which turnoff goes to the zoo from Highway 163?
5. Which highway runs east and west?
6. Which direction does Interstate 5 run?

INTERVIEW

1. How often do you drive on the freeway (expressway, highway)?
2. Do you like to drive on the freeway? Why? Why not?

BUS INFORMATION

Bus Company
Operator: May I help you?
        A: Can you tell me which bus to take downtown?

Bus Company
Operator: Where are you calling from?
        A: I'm at the corner of Linda Vista Road and Ulric Street.

Bus Company
Operator: You can catch the bus right there. Take either the number 4 or the H bus.
        A: Do I need to transfer?

Bus Company
Operator: No, you don't. Either bus goes directly to town.
        A: What time does the bus leave?

Bus Company
Operator: On the hour and the half-hour.
        A: How long does it take to get to town?

Bus Company
Operator: It takes about 30 minutes.
        A: How much is the fare?

Bus Company
Operator: It's $1.00, unless you have a monthly pass. You must have the exact change or a $1 bill.
        A: Thank you.

PRACTICE

Can you tell me which bus to take downtown?
I want to know which bus to take downtown.
                plane to take to San Francisco.
                train to take to Los Angeles.
                turnoff to take to go downtown.

Which bus do I take downtown?
     plane   to San Francisco?
Take either the number 4 or the 25 bus.
             80   60

What time does the bus leave?
              train depart?
              plane arrive?

How long does it take to get downtown?
                 drive to Mexico?
                 fly to New York?

It takes 30 minutes.
        half an hour.
        quite a while.
        a few minutes.
        several hours.

A: Excuse me. I want to get off on University Avenue. Does the bus stop near there?

Driver: There's a bus stop one block before.

A: Would you please tell me when we get there?

Driver: Yes, I'll be glad to.

A: Can you tell me where I would get off to transfer to the H bus?

Driver: Get off on First Street and cross the street. Keep the transfer to show the driver.

A: Thank you.

Pair Practice: Sit in pairs and practice the following conversation. Student A makes up the questions that go with the answers. Student B answers the questions.

EXAMPLE: Student A: What bus do I take to go downtown?
Student B: Take the number 25 bus downtown.

A: _____

B: Take the number 25 bus downtown.

A: _____

B: It leaves every half hour.

A: _____

B: It takes about 20 minutes.

A: _____

B: $1.00 one way.

A: _____

B: You're welcome.

GROSSMONT CENTER, TO SAN DIEGO STATE UNIVERSITY, MISSION VALLEY
FASHION VALLEY, MISSION BEACH AND PACIFIC BEACH

MONDAY THROUGH FRIDAY SCHEDULE

Leave Grossmont Center	Due Jackson Dr. & Lake Murray Blvd.	Due College Ave. & Montezuma	Due Fashion Valley	Due Mission Blvd. & W. Mission Bay Dr.	Arrive Mission Blvd. & Sapphire
6:20	6:27	6:40	6:55	7:07	7:15
. . .	. . .	7:32	7:47	7:59	8:07
7:25	7:32	7:45	8:00	8:12	8:20
. . .	. . .	8:28	8:43	8:55	9:07
8:37	8:44	8:57	9:12	9:24	9:36
. . .	. . .	9:27	9:42	9:54	10:06
9:37	9:44	9:57	10:12	10:24	10:36
. . .	. . .	10:27	10:42	10:54	11:06
10:37	10:44	10:57	11:12	11:24	11:36
. . .	. . .	11:27	11:42	11:54	12:06
11:37	11:44	11:57	12:12	12:24	12:36
. . .	. . .	12:27	12:42	12:54	1:06
12:37	12:44	12:57	1:12	1:24	1:36
. . .	. . .	1:27	1:42	1:54	2:06
1:37	1:44	1:57	2:12	2:24	2:36
. . .	. . .	2:27	2:44	2:56	3:06
2:37	2:44	2:57	3:14	3:26	3:36
. . .	. . .	3:27	3:44	3:56	4:06
3:37	3:44	3:57	4:14	4:26	4:36
. . .	. . .	4:27	4:44	4:56	5:06
4:37	4:44	4:57	5:14	5:26	5:36
. . .	. . .	5:27	5:44	5:56	6:06
5:37	5:44	5:57	6:11	6:23	6:33
6:37	6:44	6:56	7:10	7:22	7:32
7:32	7:39	7:51	8:05	8:17	8:27
8:36	8:43	8:55	9:09	9:21	9:31
9:31	9:38	9:50	10:04	10:16	10:26
10:05	10:12	10:24	10:38	10:50	11:00

Study the bus schedule above to answer the following questions.

1. How long does it take to go from Grossmont Center to Fashion Valley if you leave Grossmont Center at 7:25 in the morning?
2. How many buses leave Grossmont Center before 12:00 noon?
3. If you have to be at Fashion Valley at 12:00 noon, what's the latest bus you can take from Grossmont Center?
4. If you leave College Avenue at 10:27, what time will you arrive at Mission Boulevard and Sapphire?
5. If you leave Grossmont Center at 10:37 in the morning to go to Fashion Valley but you miss the bus, how long do you have to wait for the next bus?

AT THE BUS DEPOT

Clerk: May I help you?
A: Yes. I'd like two tickets on the next bus to Portland, please.
Clerk: One way or round-trip?
You save 10% on a round-trip ticket.
A: Then two round-trip tickets, please.
B: Is this an express bus?
Clerk: Yes, it goes straight through to Portland. No stops. Do you have any baggage to check?
B: We have one suitcase.
Clerk: Write your name on this tag, please. Don't you want to check that one, too?
B: No. I want to hand-carry this one.
Clerk: Put this tag on your bag and keep the claim check. The bus will be loading at the west end of the depot in 15 minutes. Have a good trip.
A: Thank you.

PRACTICE

I'd like two tickets, please.
    a schedule,
    my baggage,
      luggage,
      suitcases,
      claim check,

I want to hand-carry this one.
    plan   check
    intend tag
            send

_____ to: (Your city)	One way	Round-trip	Leave	Arrive
City A	13.35	25.35	10:15	12:20
City B	12.90	19.50	7:30	10:45
City C	14.10	19.95	8:00	10:20
City D	63.45	120.55	7:00 A.M.	6:45 P.M.

Pair Practice: Sit in pairs and ask each other questions using the information on the chart above.

EXAMPLE: Student A: How much is a one-way ticket from here to City A?
Student B: $13.35.
Student A: How much is a round-trip ticket? (And so on)

INTERVIEW

1. Have you ever taken a bus out of town?
2. Where did you go?
3. How long did it take?
4. Was it expensive?
5. Did you enjoy the trip? Why or why not?
6. Did you have any problems?

Take-home Assignment:

1. Find out the name and telephone number of a long-distance bus company in your city.
2. Choose three cities you would like to visit.
3. Call the bus station and find out the fares, departure times, and arrival times.
4. Write the information on the chart below, and bring it to class.
5. Share the information with the students in your class.

	Destination	One-Way Fare	Round-Trip Fare	Leave	Arrive
	Example: Los Angeles	12.50	19.95	9:15	12:00
1					
2					
3					
4					

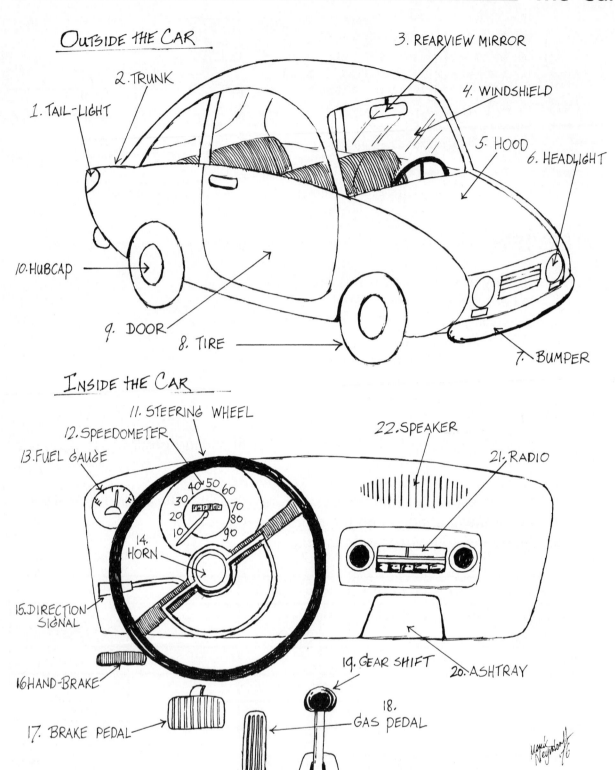

OUTSIDE THE CAR

3. REARVIEW MIRROR

2. TRUNK

4. WINDSHIELD

1. TAIL-LIGHT

5. HOOD

6. HEADLIGHT

10. HUBCAP

9. DOOR

8. TIRE

7. BUMPER

INSIDE THE CAR

11. STEERING WHEEL

12. SPEEDOMETER

22. SPEAKER

13. FUEL GAUGE

21. RADIO

14. HORN

15. DIRECTION SIGNAL

16 HAND-BRAKE

19. GEAR SHIFT

20. ASHTRAY

17. BRAKE PEDAL

18. GAS PEDAL

HAVE IT SERVICED

A: What can I do for you today?
B: We're going to go on a trip.
   I want the car to be in good shape.
   Could you check the oil and water, please?
A: Have you had any special problems?
B: Yes, the red oil light comes on sometimes.
A: You might be low on oil, or it might be a loose wire. I'll check it for you. You should probably have it serviced, too.
B: What does that include?
A: It includes a lube job, oil change, and a transmission check.
B: Can you give me an estimate of the total cost?
A: It will be between $50 and $75.
B: OK. I'll think about it. I can't leave it today. I'm in a hurry.

PRACTICE

We're going to go on a long trip.
                take a vacation.
                visit some friends.
                move to Texas.

I'll check it for you.
    replace
    fix
    repair

The red oil light comes on.
    brake light light comes on.
    generator light comes on.
    brakes grab.
    engine heats up.
    engine knocks.
    car won't start.
    car vibrates.
    signal light doesn't work.
    radiator boils over.

You might be low on oil.
    need new wiring.
    brake fluid.
    a new regulator.
    new brake shoes.
    a tune-up.
    a new battery.
    air in the tires.
    have a loose wire.
    a water leak.

I'll call you if it's going to be more expensive.
                difficult.

You should probably have it serviced.
    repaired.
    fixed.
    checked.
    adjusted.

INTERVIEW

1. Have you ever had problems with your car?
2. When?
3. What happened?
4. Who fixed it?
5. Was it expensive?
6. Did you have any problems? (Please explain.)

SELF-SERVICE GAS STATION

A: Yes?
B: Ten dollars unleaded on number 6, please.
A: What pump?
B: Number 6.
B: (After trying pump) Excuse me, number 6 isn't working.
A: Did you lift up the nozzle hook?
B: Yes.
A: Then wait a minute. Start pumping after the dial resets to zero.
B: OK. I see now.

PRACTICE

Start pumping *after* the dial resets.
Lower the hook *after* you pump the gas.
Replace the cap *after* you pump the gas.

Pay the cashier *before* you pump the gas.
Lift up the hook *before* you pump the gas.
Stop the engine *before* you pump the gas.

INTERVIEW

1. Do you have a car?
2. When you stop for gas, who pumps the gas?
3. In your country, who pumped the gas?
4. Which do you prefer—self-serve or full serve? Why?
5. Do you know anybody who is a service station attendant here in the U.S.?
   Does he or she like the job?
   How much does a service station attendant earn?

NO SMOKING. TURN OFF THE ENGINE

1. Remove nozzle.
2. Place nozzle in car fuel tank.
3. Lift nozzle hook.
4. Wait for computer to reset to zero.
5. Dispense product.
6. After delivery, lower hook and replace nozzle.

Caution: Do not lower nozzle hook until you finish delivery.

Study the directions above to decide if the following statements are true or false.

1. Lift the nozzle hook after you place the nozzle in the tank.
2. Lower the hook before you dispense the gas.
3. Wait for the computer to reset to zero after you dispense the product.
4. Dispense the gas after you lift the nozzle hook.

Pair Practice: Student A asks the questions. Student B refers to the directions above to answer the questions.

1. What do I do first?
2. What do I do before I lift the nozzle hook?
3. What do I do after I dispense the gas?
4. What do I do after I lift the nozzle hook?

A BLOWOUT

The dialogue below is not finished. Decide what could be added to complete the dialogue. Many different answers are possible.

A: What's the matter? You look upset.
B: Wow, I really had a close call today.
A: What happened?
B: I was driving south on Highway 163 when I had a blowout.
A: What did you do?
B: I took my foot off the brake and tried to steer to the side of the road, but the car began to skid.
A: You're lucky no one hit you.
B: I sure am. Fortunately, I pulled over before anything happened.
A: After you stopped, what did you do?

B: _____

_____

PRACTICE

I was driving south when I had a blowout.
When I had a blowout, I was driving south.
                    turning a corner.
                    parking.
                    speeding.
                    coming down the hill.

I pulled over before anything happened.
               the car started to skid.
               I lost control of the car.

After you stopped, what did you do?
          pulled over
          got out of the car

INTERVIEW

1. Have you ever had a blowout or flat tire?
2. What did you do?

1. What were the young man and the woman doing? What was the man in front doing?

2. What happened? Why? What were they doing while he was signaling?

3. What happened next? What did he tell the police officer? What was the police officer doing while the drivers were talking? What do you think each of the drivers did next?

4. Where do you think the two drivers met next? What do you think happened between the two meetings? What do you think the young man is giving to the other driver?

INTERVIEW

Have you ever had a car accident, or do you know anyone who has had a car accident?

a. Were you driving?
b. What were you doing when it happened?
c. What happened?
d. Whose fault was it?

e. Did the police come?
f. What did the police do?
g. How did you feel after the accident?
h. Did you have any problems after the accident?

WHAT TO DO AFTER AN ACCIDENT

In the Event of an Accident:

1. Call or have someone notify police immediately.

2. See a doctor even for simple injuries.

3. Get names and license numbers, including witnesses (don't talk to or give any information to anyone but the police.)

4. Unless immediate medical care is needed, do not leave scene of accident until police arrive.

5. Report accident to your insurance company, and make no statement to anyone except police.

6. Sign no documents (except if police issue you a ticket).

7. Make notes; if possible, take pictures to relate later to the accident and injuries (don't try to remember details).

Study the information above to decide if the following statements are true or false.

1. If you have an accident, you should remove your car from the area as soon as possible.
2. You should notify your insurance company of the accident as soon as possible.
3. If the police give you a ticket, you should sign it.
4. It is not necessary to go to the doctor if you are hurt only a little.
5. It is important to get the license numbers of any witnesses who saw the accident.
6. You shouldn't explain the accident to anyone but the police.
7. After an accident, you should call your lawyer before you call the police.

INTERVIEW

Sit with a student from another country, if possible. Discuss the questions below.

1. Is insurance required to drive a car in your country? Is insurance available? Is it optional? Is it expensive?
2. In your country, does everyone who drives have insurance?
3. What could happen in the United States if someone drives without insurance?

SPEEDING

A police officer stops a student for speeding. The police car flashes its lights. The student pulls over.

Student: Did I do something wrong, officer?
What's the matter?
Police: Well, don't you know that this is a 45-mile zone and you were doing 55?
Student: Oh, I'm sorry. I didn't realize I was going so fast.
Police: Let me see your driver's license. How long have you been in this country?
Student: Only six months, sir.
Police: I'll give you a warning this time, but don't let it happen again. Watch the signs from now on.
Student: Thank you. I will.

PRACTICE

Don't you know that this is a 45-mile zone?
        school zone?
        business district?

Yes, I know.
No, I didn't know.

Didn't you know that this was a no-parking area?
         no-waiting

Didn't you see the sign?
    have your license?
    fasten your seatbelt?

Don't let it happen again.
     upset you.
     worry you.

I didn't realize I was speeding.
       going so fast.
       driving so slow.

You were going 70.
   speeding.
   driving too slow.
   making an illegal left turn.
   tailgating.

INTERVIEW

1. Do you have a car?
2. Do you have a driver's license?
3. Do you have insurance?
4. Have you ever gotten a ticket?
   What for?

A: What's bothering you today?
B: Remember the speeding ticket I got last week, when I was doing 70 in a 55-mile zone?
A: Yes. Let me see, did you get the bail notice?
B: Yes, but it says I have to pay $50, and I don't have that much cash. What am I going to do?
A: Take it easy. If you appear in court on the date listed and explain your problem, the judge might reduce the fine or even drop the charges.
B: Really?
A: It's possible. It all depends on the number of tickets you have gotten and how fast you were going.

PRACTICE

What's bothering you today?
        disturbing
        upsetting
It depends on the number of tickets.
                kind of crime.
                charges.
I will have to pay $50.
            a fine.
            go to court.
                    driving school.
                    jail.
What am I going to do?
                wear?
                say?
                tell them?
                have to pay?
The judge might reduce the fine.
            drop the charges.
            let you off.
            fine you.
            suspend your license.
            put you in jail.

INTERVIEW

1. What are other reasons that people get tickets?
2. What can happen to someone who gets a ticket?
   What can happen to someone who gets more than one ticket in one year?
3. What can you do if you can't pay the fine?
4. What happens in your country when people don't drive according to the laws?

FILLING OUT A DRIVER'S LICENSE APPLICATION

John Allen Brown lives at 2130 Jackson Ave., Los Angeles, CA 92005. He was born on June 11, 1949. He is 5'7'' tall and weighs 165 pounds. He has brown hair and blue eyes. He has never had a driver's license before, and he doesn't wear glasses. He needs a driver's license in order to drive his car to work every day.

Please fill out John Brown's application form for him.

Print complete name _____

                       First   Middle   Last

Mailing address _____

City _____ Zip code _____

Residence address _____

City _____ County _____ Zip code _____

Sex _____ Color hair _____ Color eyes _____

Height _____   Weight _____

Birth date _____ / _____ / _____

             Month   Day   Year

Have you applied for a license under a former or different name (including maiden name) within the past 10 years?   Yes ___ No ___

Have you had your driving privilege canceled, refused, suspended, or revoked in this or any other state?   Yes ___ No ___

Have you held a valid driver's license in another state or country within the past 3 years?   Yes ___ No ___

When did or will the license

If yes, where? _____ expire? _____

Do you have any physical or mental disease, disorder, or disability that could interfere with your ability to operate a motor vehicle?   Yes ___ No ___

Do you wear contact lenses?   Yes ___ No ___

Do you intend to: drive motorcycles?   Yes ___ No ___

           drive buses?   Yes ___ No ___

           operate or tow vehicles weighing 6,000 lb. gross or over?   Yes ___ No ___

A: I'm calling about the Toyota for sale.
B: Yes?
A: Have you sold it yet?
B: Not yet.
A: Is it an automatic or stick shift?
B: Stick shift.
A: How long have you owned the car?
B: Six years. I'm the original owner.
A: How many miles does it have on it?
B: Only 40,000.
A: May I see the car?
B: Sure. When can you come?
A: Is this evening OK?
B: Yes. I'll be here.
A: OK, thanks. My name is John Lee. I'll stop by around 8:00 P.M.
B: See you then.

Pair Practice: Practice the conversation below with your teacher and then with another student. Student A asks the questions; student B answers them.

EXAMPLE: Student A: How many miles does the car have on it?
               Student B: The car has 9,000 miles on it.

A: _____

B: The car has 9,000 miles on it.

A: _____

B: It's a Mustang.

A: _____

B: The car has had two owners.

A: _____

B: The blue book price, established by car dealers, is $2,000.

A: _____

B: Yes, it's an automatic.

A: _____

B: It has AM/FM radio, air conditioning, and a heater.

A: _____

B: Yes, the tires are excellent.

A: _____

B: It's a 1979.

A: _____

B: It has a rebuilt engine.

A: _____

B: Yes, there is a guarantee for the first 6,000 miles.

1.
> Toyota '78 5 spd superb cond. Radials air am/fm 2 dr new eng $1795/ofr P/pty 473-5869.

2.
> VW '76 Bug like nu low mi am/fm stereo a/c ylw many xtras $1995 725LVI Co. car 627-3068.

3.
> Buick '70 Riviera $975 or best offer Xnt cond orig pr/pty. 788-4621.

4.
> Ford '83 Mustang stk 7000 mi warr offer 867 NKB Pr. Pty 213-4750.

5.
> Ford '81 LTD wgn V8 (780 LYS) mk mo pymts Keystone Ford.

Study the classified ads above to answer the following questions.

Car 1. What does cond. mean?
     What are radials?
     What does am/fm mean?
       2 dr
       new eng
       p/pty
     Might the owner sell for less than $1795?
     What is extra on the car?

Car 2. What does a/c mean?
       xtras
       low mi
       725 LVI
     What color is the car?
Car 3. What does orig pr/pty mean?
       warr
Car 4. What does stk mean?
       xlnt cond.
Car 5. What does wgn mean?
       mk mo pymts mean?

1. Which ad tells you that the car has had only one owner?

2. What is the newest car advertised?

Study the ads to find out whether the statements below are true or false.

1. The VW Bug has air conditioning.
2. A used car company is selling the Ford '83 Mustang.
3. The Toyota is yellow.
4. It is possible that you can buy the car in ad 1 for less than $1795.
5. The listed price of the Ford Mustang is $7,000. Which car would you buy? Why?

What questions should a person ask to obtain the following information?

1. General Information

   Make and model of the car
   Year (age of the car)
   Number of miles driven
   Average miles per gallon
   Price

2. Accessories

   Automatic transmission or stick shift
   Air conditioning and/or heater
   Power steering and brakes
   Kind of radio (standard AM/FM or stereo)

3. Condition of Car

   Outside appearance (paint, scratches, nicks, and so on)
   Under fender (check to see if there has been body work)
   Under hood, check for the following:
      General condition of engine and battery
      Frayed cables
      Worn belts
      Radiator damage or leaks that have been repaired

4. Things to Do

   Listen to engine.
   Slam doors to see if anything is loose.
   Road test: Hit brakes.
   Check speed of pick-up.
   See how car corners.
   Listen for strange noises.
   Check tires.

Role-Play

Student A: Pretend you are buying a car. Call up and ask about the ad listed below. Student B: Look at the ad below and answer the questions that your partner asks.

Dodge '78 6 cyl standard, good eng, body, and paint. New brakes, trans., $1050 or best offer. 488-3063

INTERVIEW

1. If you could buy a new car next week, what kind would you buy? What model?
2. Why do you like this kind of car?

chapter 5

HOUSING

COMPETENCY OBJECTIVES

On completion of this unit the students will show orally, in writing, or through demonstration that they are able to use language needed in the following situations:

A. LOCATING HOUSING

- State needs and ask specific questions about housing.
- Interpret classified housing ads.
- Interpret and complete a rental application.

B. COMMUNICATING WITH NEIGHBORS

- Ask to borrow basic tools or household items from a neighbor.
- Make complaints and respond appropriately to complaints from neighbors.

C. HOUSING REGULATIONS AND MAINTENANCE PROBLEMS

- Read and interpret standard rules for renting.
- Explain the nature or cause of a household problem and arrange for needed repairs.
- Read and interpret a label on a can of insect spray.
- Arrange for starting or stopping utility services.

NEEDS ASSESSMENT EXERCISE _____

HOUSING

I need to improve my English so that I can

_____ state my needs and ask questions to rent a house or an apartment.

_____ read and understand newspaper ads for apartments and houses.

_____ read and fill out an application to rent an apartment or house.

_____ talk with my neighbors (get information, borrow something, complain about something).

_____ describe household problems and get needed repairs or services.

_____ read and understand tenant (renter's) rules and responsibilities.

_____ arrange for starting or stopping utility services (telephone, gas, electricity).

LOOKING FOR AN APARTMENT

A: I was told that you have an apartment for rent.
B: Yes, we do.
A: How many bedrooms does it have?
B: It has two bedrooms, and it's furnished.
A: How much is the rent?
B: It's $595.
A: Are the utilities included?
B: The water is included. You pay for the gas and electricity.
A: Are any deposits required?
B: Yes—a $200 cleaning deposit is required.
A: Do you rent month-to-month or by a lease?
B: We have a month-to-month agreement.
A: Are pets allowed?
B: No, I'm sorry they aren't.
A: I'm sorry. We wouldn't be interested. We have two dogs.

PRACTICE

I was told that you have an apartment for rent.
      a studio
      a duplex
      a house
      a condominium

Are the utilities included?
   gas and electricity
Is parking space
   water

Are pets allowed?

Is smoking allowed?
 barbecuing

Questions to Ask When You Rent a House or an Apartment

1. Is it furnished or unfurnished? If furnished, what is included?
2. How much is the rent? When is it due?
3. How large is it? How many rooms?
4. Is the room arrangement convenient?
5. Is the location good? Is it convenient to public transportation, work, schools, shopping?
6. What extras are available? Are utilities included or not? Are there washing facilities, parking, storage areas?
7. What are the terms? Do you sign a lease, or is it a month-to-month arrangement?
8. Are any deposits required? How much are they? Are they refundable?
9. Is the landlord willing to redecorate and pay for any necessary repairs?
10. What are the living conditions? Is the apartment on the first floor or higher? Is there an elevator or stairs? Are the tenants noisy? Is it clean?
11. Are there any restrictions on children or pets?
12. How much notice must you give before moving?

Pair Practice: Practice with your class. Then sit in pairs and ask your partner questions about his or her house or apartment. Use the words below to help you make the questions.

EXAMPLE: Student A: Do you live in an apartment or house?
Student B: I live in an apartment.
Student A: How many bedrooms does it have?

Student B: It has _____ .

1. Do you live in an apartment or house?
2. bedrooms?
3. bathrooms?
4. furnished?
5. rent?
6. utilities?
7. deposit?
8. month-to-month agreement or lease?
9. yard?
10. parking space?
11. carpeting?
12. dishwasher?
13. like your apartment or house?

North Park $445 Furn 1 BR upper, sec bldg clean, quiet, d/wshr prkng, conv loc 582-6980	Balboa Park $650 2 BR Large, no pets 295-1695 Unfurn.
$375 1 BR 1 Ba Unfurn. New Cpts, drps, pool spa, laundry 266-8668	$445 2 BR Unfurn 1 BA patio, pool new cpt. dwshr AC no pets 440-2423
North Park $535 2 BR 1 BA stove dwshr, refrig. pet OK, new paint 566-8462 unfurn.	Linda Vista Unfurn. 3 BR 1 Ba large yd. lndry facils 292-1643 $600

Study the housing ads above to answer the following questions.

1. If you need a furnished apartment, which number will you call?
2. Which ads state that no pets are allowed?
3. Which number will you call if you need more than two bedrooms?
4. If you want an apartment with a dishwasher, which number will you call?
5. If you want an apartment with a yard, which number will you call?
6. What is the cheapest two bedroom apartment available in the ads?

Matching Exercise: Write the letter of the correct abbreviation next to each word.

_____	1. Bedroom(s)	a.	cpt
_____	2. parking	b.	drps
_____	3. convenient	c.	Ba
_____	4. location	d.	BR
_____	5. Bathroom	e.	AC
_____	6. Unfurnished	f.	yd
_____	7. carpet	g.	dwshr
_____	8. drapes	h.	prkng
_____	9. dishwasher	i.	unfurn
_____	10. air conditioning	j.	lndry
_____	11. yard	k.	loc
_____	12. laundry	l.	conv

TALKING WITH NEIGHBORS

A: Sorry to bother you.
B: No problem. What can I do for you?
A: May I borrow a hammer? I want to hang a picture, and I can't find mine.
B: Sure. Just a minute. I'll get it.
A: Thanks. I'll bring it back as soon as I finish.
B: Take your time.

PRACTICE

May I borrow a hammer?
     wrench?
     screwdriver?
     ladder?
     cup of sugar?
       flour?
Can you lend me some pliers?
       scissors?
       tape?
I want to hang a picture.
   fix my sink.
   make a cake.
   fix my smoke alarm.

Pair Practice: Practice with your class. Then sit in pairs and practice the following conversation by substituting the words below.

A: Sorry to bother you.
B: No problem. What can I do for you?

A: May I borrow a _____ 1 ?

 I want to _____ 2 .

B: Sure.

A: Thanks. I'll bring it back _____ 3 .

B: Take your time.

1. wrench	1. ladder
2. fix my bathroom sink	2. change a light bulb
3. this afternoon	3. in 15 minutes
1. a cup of sugar	1. a shovel
2. make a cake	2. plant some vegetables
3. in a few minutes	3. tonight

A: Hello.

B: Hello. I'm _____ , your neighbor. Sorry to bother you, but could you please keep the noise down a little? My children can't sleep.

A: Oh, I am sorry. I didn't know we were so loud.

B: Thank you. I appreciate that.

PRACTICE

I am sorry to bother you.
                 disturb you.
                 interrupt you.

Could you please keep the noise down?
                    turn down your stereo?
                    take your clothes out of the dryer?
                    not park in my space?
                    keep your dog out of my yard?

Pair Practice:

A: Hello. I'm _____ , your neighbor. Sorry to bother you, but could you please keep the noise down a little? My children can't sleep.

B: Sorry. If you don't like it, you can move out.

(If your neighbor said this to you, what would you say next? What would you do? What else could you do?)

A: _____

INTERVIEW

1. Do you know your neighbors?
2. Tell me about them. Do they have children? Are they quiet? Where are they from?
3. What do you like about your neighbors?
4. What don't you like about your neighbors?
5. Have you ever complained to a neighbor about something? What did they say?
6. Has a neighbor ever complained to you? What did you say?

Pair Practice: Practice the dialogue below by substituting problems 1 through 5. Student A makes the complaint, and student B responds to the complaint. Practice with your class first. Then practice with a partner.

A: Hello.

B: I'm _____ , your neighbor. Sorry to bother

you, but _____ .

Could you _____ ?

A: _____ .

Problems:

1. Your stereo is too loud.
2. You have parked in my place.
3. Your dog is in my yard.
4. Your clothes are still in the dryer.
5. Your son is throwing rocks at the other children.
6. Your trash has spilled on the street.

Rent must be paid in advance.

Do not keep dogs, cats, or birds on premises.

No loud talking, unnecessary noises, or boisterous conduct is permitted at any time.

Children are not permitted to play in halls and entrances.

Vocal or instrumental music, radio, or TV programs are not permitted before 8 A.M. or after 10 P.M. or continuously.

Premises cannot be sublet without written consent of the management.

All doors must be locked during absence of tenants and kept closed at all times.

Management will not be responsible for lost or missing articles.

Tenancy may be terminated only by a 30-day written notice of intention to so terminate.

Management has the right to enter premises for inspection and to show premises for rental and for sale of same.

The use of gasoline for any purpose inside this building is strictly prohibited.

Tenants are requested not to drive tacks, nails, or screws anywhere inside or outside the premises.

Garbage cans, milk bottles, brooms, mops, and so forth must be kept inside out of view. Hang nothing on fences or hedges.

Expense or damage caused by stopping of waste pipes or overflow from bathtubs, closets, wash basins, or sinks must be paid for by tenant.

Any damages to premises or to furnishings must be paid for by tenant.

Electric light bulbs must be replaced by tenant.

Furniture or utensils belonging in these quarters must not be loaned without the consent of the manager.

Television antenna may not be placed on the roof without written consent of the management and must be installed and removed only by a licensed television installer. Upon removal of television antenna, tenant will be held liable for any damages to the roof.

Comply with city ordinances and state and national laws.

These premises must be vacated by 12 noon on day tenancy expires.

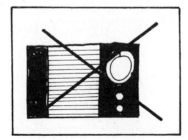

NO NOISE AFTER 10

UNDERSTANDING RENTAL RULES

Study the house rules on the previous page and mark the statements below true or false. Be prepared to read the rule that supports your answer.

_____ **1.** Pets are allowed.

_____ **2.** Playing stereo music is not permitted after 10 P.M.

_____ **3.** Tenants are allowed to put nails in the walls to hang pictures.

_____ **4.** The apartment manager has the right to enter your apartment to show it to a future tenant.

_____ **5.** Hanging laundry on the fence to dry is not allowed.

_____ **6.** A TV antenna may be placed on the roof with the approval of the manager.

_____ **7.** If you want to go on a long trip and rent your apartment to a friend, you must make the arrangements with your friend only.

_____ **8.** Children are not allowed in the building.

_____ **9.** If the toilet overflows, the tenant must pay for the damages.

_____ **10.** The manager will provide electric light bulbs if some burn out.

_____ **11.** If you plan to move out, you should give notice to your manager at least 15 days before you plan to move.

_____ **12.** Damages to furniture must be paid for by the tenant.

APARTMENT PROBLEM

A: May I please speak to the manager?
B: This is the manager.

A: This is _____ in apartment 26.
   Sorry to bother you, but I have a problem in my apartment.
B: What's the matter?
A: There are a lot of cockroaches in the kitchen and bathroom.
   It's really bad.
B: Did you spray?
A: Yes. I tried that, but it didn't get rid of them. Can you
   call someone to spray the whole building?
B: Sorry. We only spray every six months.
A: When will they spray again?
B: In a couple of months.
A: Is there any possibility of spraying a little earlier than that?
B: I'll think about it and let you know.
A: Thank you. I appreciate your help.

PRACTICE

What's the matter? There are a lot of cockroaches.
                                        mice.
                                        bugs.
                                        rats.
                                        ants.

The faucets are dripping.
     pipes are leaking.
     roof is leaking.
     paint is chipping.
     toilet is overflowing.
The toilet doesn't flush.
     sink doesn't drain.
     bathtub doesn't drain.
The carpet is torn.
     drapes are torn.
     carpet is stained.
     drapes are stained.
The stove doesn't work.
     oven
     heater
     refrigerator
     freezer
     disposal
The pilot light goes out.
The hot water runs out.
The bulb is burned out.
The outlet is broken.

Pair Practice: Discuss the problems in this house with your teacher. Then sit with another student and practice a conversation calling a manager to complain about the problems. Use the conversation on the opposite page as an example.

INTERVIEW

1. Have you ever had a problem in your apartment or house?
2. What happened?
3. Did you call the manager to fix it?
4. Did the manager take care of the problem?
5. Who paid for the repairs?
6. Do you have any problems now?
7. What can you do if you have a housing problem and the manager won't fix it?

LIFE SKILL READING

READING AN INSECTICIDE LABEL

BLACK ANT AND ROACH KILLER

DIRECTIONS:

1. Do not spray near open flame.
2. Do not spray near children.
3. Hold container in upright position.
4. Shake well before each use.
5. Hold container 6 to 12 inches from the surface and spray until surface is wet.
6. Keep out of reach of children.

WARNING—COMBUSTIBLE MIXTURE

Study the directions above to answer the question below.

Which of the following statements is true?

a. You need to use a brush to apply this.
b. You must hold the can at least 6 inches from the area to be sprayed.
c. You should hold the can with the top pointing down when you begin spraying.
d. Spray the surface for about 12 minutes.

ESTABLISHING TELEPHONE SERVICE

A: May I help you?
B: Yes, I would like to have my phone connected.
A: Is your apartment already wired for telephone service?
B: Yes, it is.
A: Do you have your own telephones?
B: No, I don't. I've just moved here from Mexico.
A: We can activate your phone line, but you will have to purchase your own telephones.
B: Is a deposit required?
A: Yes, you must pay a deposit unless someone who has a phone signs a form to guarantee your account.
B: Thank you. I'll call back later to make the arrangements.

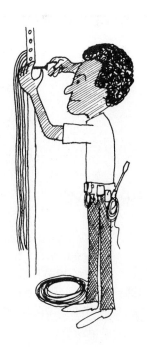

PRACTICE

I would like to have my phone connected.
   have to   house wired for service.
   want to   phone disconnected.

You must pay a deposit unless someone signs for you.
                                  guarantees your account.
                      you qualify for credit.
                          have been a customer before.

You can't call unless you have a telephone.
           have service unless you pay the deposit.
                  you qualify for credit.

You have to purchase your own telephones.
           complete a credit application.
           have someone guarantee your bills.
           pay a deposit.

INTERVIEW

Do you have a telephone?
What kinds of service do you have?
What are the rates?

CALLING THE PLUMBER

A: I'm calling to get some advice.
B: What seems to be the problem?
A: We can't turn the water off completely. The faucet keeps on dripping. It's been that way since Tuesday.
B: Oh, that sounds like it's just a washer.
   You can buy a new one in any hardware store, and just change it yourself.
A: I'm not very good at that kind of thing, but I'll try.
   How much will you charge if I can't figure it out?
B: Labor is $35 an hour plus any charge for parts.
A: Thank you, anyway. I'm sure I can do it myself.
   If I can't, I'll get a friend to help.

PRACTICE

It's been that way since Tuesday.
                       last year.
                       January.
                       I first came here.
                       he came.

It's been that way for two days.
                       three months.
                       the last week.
                       a long time.

If I can't figure it out, how much will you charge?
                       when can I call you?
                       when can you come?

If I can't, I'll get a friend.   I can do it myself.

         ask for help.   He   _____

         try another way.   She   _____

         call you.   You   _____

         call the landlord.   They   _____

INTERVIEW

1. Have you ever had a plumbing problem in your apartment or house?
   If yes, who fixed it?
   How much did it cost?
2. Have you ever tried to fix something yourself?
   What happened?

Group Activity: Find someone who has had the following things done by asking each

person a question beginning with *Have you ever had a* _____

_____ ?

If the answer is yes, ask the person to sign his or her name on the line, and ask another question beginning with a question word. (When? Why? How much?)

EXAMPLE: Student A: Have you ever had a carpet cleaned?
      Student B: Yes, I have.
      Student A: (*When*) When did you have it done?
      Student B: I had it done six months ago.

FINE SOMEONE WHO HAS HAD A

  1.   carpet cleaned _____

  2.   roof repaired _____

  3.   house painted _____

  4.   window replaced _____

  5.   faucet fixed _____

  6.   sofa reupholstered _____

  7.   drain cleaned _____

  8.   cable TV installed _____

  9.   lock changed _____

  10.   house fumigated _____

FILLING IN A RENT APPLICATION FORM

Discuss this rent application with your teacher. Then complete it by filling in the blank spaces.

APPLICATION TO RENT
(all sections must be completed)

Individual applications required from each adult occupant.

NAME		SOCIAL SECURITY NUMBER

DATE OF BIRTH	DRIVER'S LICENSE NO	STATE	HOME PHONE NUMBER

COMPLETE SECTIONS 2 & 3 ONLY IF YOU HAVE LIVED AT ADDRESS #1 FOR LESS THAN 5 YEARS

1 PRESENT ADDRESS

DATE IN	DATE OUT	OWNER/MGR NAME	OWNER MGR PHONE NO

REASON FOR MOVING

2 PREVIOUS ADDRESS

DATE IN	DATE OUT	OWNER/MGR NAME	OWNER/MGR PHONE NO

REASON FOR MOVING

3 NEXT PREVIOUS ADDRESS

DATE IN	DATE OUT	OWNER/MGR NAME	OWNER/MGR PHONE NO

REASON FOR MOVING

PROPOSED OCCUPANTS	NAME	AGE	NAME	AGE
LIST ALL IN ADDITION TO YOURSELF				

WILL YOU HAVE PETS?	DESCRIBE	WILL YOU HAVE LIQUID FILLED FURNITURE?	DESCRIBE

COMPLETE SECTION B ONLY IF YOU HAVE BEEN WITH PRESENT EMPLOYER FOR LESS THAN 5 YEARS

A

PRESENT OCCUPATION	EMPLOYER NAME
HOW LONG WITH THIS EMPLOYER?	EMPLOYER ADDRESS
NAME OF YOUR SUPERVISOR	EMPLOYER PHONE NO

B

PRIOR OCCUPATION	EMPLOYER NAME
HOW LONG WITH THIS EMPLOYER?	EMPLOYER ADDRESS
NAME OF YOUR SUPERVISOR	EMPLOYER PHONE NO

CURRENT GROSS INCOME	CHECK ONE		
	WEEK	MON	YR
$ PER			

PLEASE LIST ALL OF YOUR FINANCIAL OBLIGATIONS BELOW

NAME OF YOUR BANK	BRANCH OR ADDRESS	ACCOUNT NUMBER	
		CHECKING	
		SAVINGS	

NAME OF CREDITOR	ADDRESS	PHONE NO	MO PYMT AMT

chapter 6

SHOPPING AND BANKING

COMPETENCY OBJECTIVES

On completion of this unit the students will show orally, in writing, or through demonstration that they are able to use language needed in the following situations:

A. CLOTHING

- Make and respond to compliments about clothing.
- Identify others by description of clothing.

B. SHOPPING

- Express the need to return or exchange items of clothing, stating the reason for dissatisfaction.
- Ask and answer questions regarding methods of purchasing clothing (layaway, charge accounts, payments by check).
- Ask questions in order to purchase items at a garage sale.
- Interpret furniture ads in the newspaper.

C. CLOTHING CARE

- Ask about and interpret oral instructions for the care of clothing.
- Interpret information on clothing labels.

D. BANKING

- Ask and answer questions in order to open a savings account.
- Ask and answer questions regarding the status of a checking account.
- Interpret a checking account deposit slip.

NEEDS ASSESSMENT EXERCISE _____

SHOPPING AND BANKING

I need to improve my English so that I can

_____ give someone a compliment about his or her clothing.

_____ identify people by describing their clothing.

_____ return or exchange an item of clothing and state the reason for the return or exchange.

_____ ask and answer questions about methods of purchasing clothing (layaway, charge account, check, cash).

_____ ask questions to purchase an item at a garage sale.

_____ read and understand ads for furniture.

_____ understand and follow instructions for the care of clothing.

_____ ask and answer questions to open a savings account.

_____ ask and answer questions about a checking account.

_____ read and understand a checking account deposit slip.

WHAT A BEAUTIFUL JACKET YOU HAVE ON TODAY ____

A: What a beautiful jacket you have on today!
B: Thank you.
A: You wear a lot of blue, don't you?
B: Yes, I like blue.
A: Why don't you wear that jacket more often?
B: Because it has to be dry cleaned, and that gets too expensive.
A: I know what you mean.

PRACTICE

(Complimenting people on their clothing)

What a beautiful jacket you have on today.   Thank you.
You look great in that jacket.
That jacket looks great on you.
I really like your jacket.

You wear a lot of blue, don't you?
        beige
        pink
        gray
        turquoise

He wears a lot of blue, doesn't he?
She

Why don't you wear that jacket more often?
          color
          outfit

It has to be dry cleaned.
      ironed.
      pressed.
      washed by hand.

Pair Practice: Use the cue words below to practice different ways of complimenting someone in your class by the clothes he or she is wearing.

EXAMPLE: What a. . . !
             What a beautiful suit you have on!

1. What a. . . .
2. You look. . . .
3. That blouse. . . .
4. I really like. . . .

BUYING JEANS

A: Good morning. May I help you?
B: Yes, I'd like to buy a pair of blue denim jeans.
A: Which style do you like?
B: I like the ones that are preshrunk.
A: What size do you wear?
B: I think I wear a 30-28.
A: Here's a pair that's on sale. You can try them on in the dressing room.
B: They're OK in the waist, but they're too short. Do you have some longer ones in the same style?
A: Try these. They aren't as dark as the other ones, but they're longer.
B: Are they the same price as the other ones?
A: No, they're $5 cheaper—$25 instead of $30.
B: Great! I'll take them.
A: Just take them to the cashier behind the counter.
B: Thank you.

PRACTICE

I'd like to buy a pair of blue denim jeans.
                    blue corduroy
                    beige cotton pants.
                    brown wool
                    brown work

I like the jeans that are preshrunk.
                    don't shrink.
                    don't have any belt loops.
                    don't fade.

Do you have some longer ones in the same style?
                    color?
                    material?
                    waist size?

They aren't as dark as the other ones.
              long
              tight
              short

What size pants do you wear?
              shirt
              blouse
              dress
              sport coat

WILL THEY SHRINK?

A: Would you like to buy those pants?
B: I think so, but let me ask you, will they shrink after I wash them?
A: No, they won't. They are preshrunk.
B: Great. I'll take them.

PRACTICE

Will they shrink after I wash them?
  shrink   dry
  fade   wash
  stretch   wear

They won't shrink.
  fade.
  stretch.
  wrinkle.

Pair Practice: Practice the conversation below with your teacher and then with a partner. Student A asks student B a question, using the words given. Student B reads the label in the box and answers the question. Then, student B asks the question, and so on.

EXAMPLE:

A: (Wash in the machine—sweater)

B:
> Hand wash cold. May be dry cleaned.
> Do not twist or wring. Reshape.
> Dry flat or dry clean.

A: Can I wash this sweater in the washing machine?
B: No, you shouldn't wash it in the machine. The label says to hand wash it.

1. A: (use bleach—jacket)

   B:
   > 100% cotton
   > Machine wash warm
   > Do not bleach.
   > Tumble dry
   > Warm iron when needed.

2. A: (Wash in the washing machine—blouse)

   B:
   > 100% cotton
   > Hand wash separately in cold water
   > Line dry
   > Warm iron
   > Do not use bleach

3. A: (Put in the dryer—shirt)

   B:
   > Machine wash cold separately
   > tumble dry cool
   > Press as needed

4. A: (Wash in the washing machine—skirt)

   B:
   > Dry clean only
   > 100% silk

UNDERSTANDING WASHING INSTRUCTIONS

1.		Hand wash cold. May be dry cleaned. Do not twist or wring. Reshape. Dry flat or dry clean.	sweater
2.		Machine wash cool. Gentle cycle, tumble dry, remove promptly. Press on wrong side with warm iron.	shirt
3.		Hand wash separately. Line dry. Use warm iron. Do not use bleach. Do not dry clean.	skirt
4.		100% cotton. Preshrunk. Machine wash, hot water. Tumble dry. Press with hot iron.	white shirt
5.		69% cotton, 31% polyester. Machine wash warm. Tumble dry, Remove immediately. Cool iron touch-up.	blue blouse

Study the clothing labels above to answer the following questions.

1. Which items must be washed by hand?

   a. 1 and 3
   b. 1 and 2
   c. 2, 4, and 5
   d. 1, 3, and 5

2. Which item has already been washed, according to the label?

   a. 1
   b. 2
   c. 4
   d. 5

3. Which item should not be dry cleaned?

   a. 1
   b. 3
   c. 2
   d. 5

4. How should the blue blouse be cleaned?

   a. Washed in the machine with hot water
   b. Hand washed
   c. Washed in the machine with cold water
   d. Washed in the machine with warm water

EXCHANGING SHOES

Clerk: May I help you?
    A: Yes, I'd like to exchange these shoes for my daughter.
       The strap broke the first time she wore them.
Clerk: Do you have the receipt?
    A: Here it is.
Clerk: I'll check to see if we have another pair.
       (A moment later) Sorry, we're all out of that style. Would you like
       to pick out something else?
    A: These look nice, and they're on sale. If they don't fit,
       I can return them, can't I?
Clerk: No, I'm sorry. Sale items cannot be returned or exchanged.
    A: Well then, I guess I'd better get a refund.

PRACTICE

If they don't fit, I can return them, can't I?
                 bring them back
                 exchange them
                 get my money back
I guess I'd better get a refund.
               look somewhere else.
               try another style.
               wait for the others to come in.

INTERVIEW

1. Have you ever exchanged an item in a store?
2. Why did you want to exchange it?
3. Did you have any problem exchanging it?
4. If you didn't have the receipt, what could you do?
5. Can you exchange purchases in your country?
    If yes, how do you do it in your country?

Pair Practice: Practice the conversation below, substituting the new words (marked 1, 2).

Student A: May I help you?

Student B: Yes. I'd like to _____ this _____ .
                              1   1

Student A: Do you have the receipt?
Student B: Yes, here it is.
Student A: What seems to be the problem?

Student B: _____ .
                2

1. return/jacket
2. The zipper doesn't work.

1. return/coat
2. Two seams are ripped.

1. exchange/dress
2. There's a stain on it.

1. exchange/shirt
2. It's the wrong size.

LAYAWAY

A: I saw the best-looking sport coat at the shopping center today.
B: What was it like?
A: It was a blue and yellow plaid that would go perfectly with my new pants.
B: Did you buy it?
A: If I had the money, I'd go back and buy it right away. It was on sale, but I'm broke this month.
B: Why don't you put it on layaway?
A: Layaway? I've never heard of that before.
B: You can pay a little down on the coat now, and they'll hold it for you until you can pay the full amount.
A: That's a great idea. I'll go back to the store tomorrow and do that.

PRACTICE

I saw the best-looking sport coat today.
                  plaid shirt
                  striped pants
                  print blouse
                  pleated skirt

It was a blue and yellow plaid that would go perfectly with my pants.
                                              nicely
                                              beautifully
                                              well

If I had the money, I'd go back and buy it.
        my credit card,
              checkbook,
    needed it,
    liked it,

They'll hold it for you until you can pay the full amount.
                              come back.
              5:00 tomorrow.

INTERVIEW

1. Have you ever put anything on layaway?
   If yes, why?
2. Is it possible to put something on layaway in your country?

Pair Practice: Practice describing each person with a partner. Use the conversation in the example as a model.

EXAMPLE: Student A: There's Bob.
           Student B: Which one is Bob?
           Student A: The boy wearing the striped T-shirt.

1. Bob

2. Dan

3. Susan

4. Joe

5. Sally

6. Mrs. Jones

CASHING A CHECK

A: Did you get the things you had on layaway?
B: No, I couldn't cash the check that Joe gave me, and I didn't have enough cash.
A: Why couldn't you cash the check? Didn't you have identification?
B: Yes, I had my driver's license and a credit card, but they wouldn't accept a two-party check. Joe made the check out to me.
A: How are you supposed to cash it, then?
B: I guess I've got to go to the bank.

PRACTICE

I couldn't cash the check that Joe gave me.
                               you sent me.
                               John wrote.
                               I received in the mail.

Didn't you have identification?
                     any cash?
                     a credit card?
                     your wallet?

How are you supposed to cash it, then?
                             get the money,
                             open an account,

INTERVIEW

1. Have you ever received a check from a friend?
   Where did you go to cash it?
   Did you have any problem cashing it?
2. If a friend gave you a check and you wanted cash instead, what would you say?
3. Did you write checks in your country?
4. Do you have a checking account in the U.S.?
5. What do you think are some advantages and disadvantages of having a checking account?

CHARGE ACCOUNT

A: You have a charge account, don't you?
B: Yes, I do, but it's not as convenient as I thought.
A: What do you mean?
B: Well, I overdid it during the holidays this year and charged over $200 worth of presents that I really couldn't afford. It's been six months, and I'm still trying to pay off the account.
A: It's only $10 a month, isn't it?
B: Yes, but I have to pay a 1.5% monthly interest charge also.
A: So, in the long run, you're paying a lot more.
B: That's right. I guess I learned the hard way.

PRACTICE

You have a charge account, don't you?
      the sales slip,
      the receipt,
      enough money,

You have a charge account, don't you?

    had   _____ ?

You will use your charge account, _____ ?

It's not as convenient as I thought.
      economical
      practical
      easy

I'm still trying to pay off the account.
                bill.
                debt.
                charges.

INTERVIEW

1. Do you have any charge accounts?
2. Are charge accounts common in your country? Why or why not?
3. What do you think are the advantages and disadvantages of having charge accounts?

IS MY ACCOUNT OVERDRAWN?

Customer: Could you please tell me what my balance is? I think my account might be overdrawn.
Teller: Just a minute. I'll look it up. (A moment later) Your balance is $3.23.
Customer: I was afraid of that. I just wrote a check for $25.00 this morning. Could I transfer some money from my savings account into my checking account?
Teller: Yes. First of all, fill out a savings withdrawal slip. Then make out a deposit slip for your checking account.
Customer: My account won't be overdrawn, will it?
Teller: Don't worry. Anything deposited before 5:00 today will be credited to your account.
Customer: That's a relief. I can't afford any extra service charges this month.

PRACTICE

My account won't be overdrawn, will it?
name   won't be misspelled, will it?
application won't be lost, will it?

It will be deposited in my account, won't it?
        credited to
        charged to

I can't afford any extra service charges this month.
        to pay for the car.
        to buy that house.

IS THIS ACCOUNT OVERDRAWN?

RECORD ALL CHARGES OR CREDITS THAT AFFECT YOUR ACCOUNT

NUMBER	DATE	DESCRIPTION OF TRANSACTION	PAYMENT/DEBIT (−)	√ T	FEE (IF ANY) (−)	DEPOSIT/CREDIT (+)	BALANCE
							$ 105.00
101	3/25	Pacific Bell	$ 25 50	$	$		79.50
102	3/27	Gas and Electric	53 00				26.50
103	3/29	Fedco	54 00				

OPENING A SAVINGS ACCOUNT

A: I'd like to open a savings account, please.
B: How much would you like to deposit?
A: To start off, I'd like to deposit $200.
B: Then you probably want the regular savings account. The minimum deposit for a money market account is $1,000.
A: OK. How often may I withdraw money?
B: You may make three withdrawals each quarter without charge. If your balance is less than $500, each additional withdrawal costs 50¢.
A: What is the interest rate?
B: It's 7 1/2% compounded daily.
A: Just think—if I had $1,000 in the bank, I would make over $70 a year in interest.

PRACTICE

I'm not sure what's best for me.
　　　　　what I should do.
　　　　　what the difference is

Fill out this deposit slip for me.
　　　　　application
　　　　　contract
　　　　　paper for the manager.
　　　　　　　for her.
　　　　　　　for them.

INTERVIEW

1. Do you have a savings account?
2. What interest rate do you earn?
3. Is it easy or difficult for you to save money? Why?
4. If someone gave you $1,000 tomorrow, what would you do with it?

Pair Practice: Practice the conversation below with your teacher first and then with a partner. Add words to the cues to make complete statements and questions.

Student A begins: I'd like to open a savings account, please.

Student A:
1. Savings account. . .
2. $200. How often. . . withdraw?
3. Interest rate?
4. How often. . .interest paid?
5. OK. That sounds fine.

Student B:
1. How much. . .deposit?
2. Three times without charge each quarter
3. 5.75%
4. each quarter
5. If you can wait a few minutes, I'll type up the forms.

LIFE SKILL READING

FILLING OUT A DEPOSIT SLIP

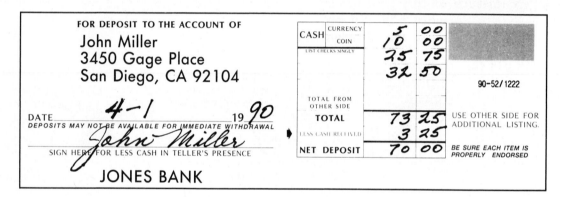

Study the checking account deposit slip above to answer the following questions.

1. How much does John want to deposit in the bank?

   a. $70.00
   b. $73.25
   c. $32.50
   d. $25.75

2. How much cash will he receive back after he presents this slip?

   a. $5.00
   b. $10.00
   c. $3.25
   d. $70.00

3. How much money in paper bills is he depositing into the bank?

   a. $5.00
   b. $10.00
   c. $15.00
   d. $70.00

GARAGE SALE _____

A: How much is this sofa?
B: $200.
A: That's a lot. The upholstery looks a little worn on the arms.
B: It's less than a year old, and we paid $700 for it.
A: Would you take $150 for it?
B: Uh, let me check with my wife.
(A moment later) How about $175?
A: I've got $170 in cash. That's all I can afford.

B: _____ .

INTERVIEW

1. Have you ever been to a garage sale?
   Did you buy anything?
   What kinds of things were for sale?
2. In the United States, is it acceptable to bargain when shopping at

   a department store?
   a swap meet or flea market?
   a car lot?
   a garage sale?
   a supermarket?
   a drug store?
   somebody's house?

3. In your country, when is it acceptable to bargain?
4. Who bargains more in your country, men or women?

Weekly Saver Newspaper

GOING OUT OF BUSINESS SALE Everything goes!! 30-50% off. $400,000 inventory must be disposed of. Bedroom sets, living room sets. 5-piece dinette sets $99.95. Full size sofa sleepers $198.88. Unfinished bunkbeds $48.88. Coffee, 2 end tables $59.95. Ortho Deluxe mattress sets, 10 year warranty. Twin $99.88. full $148.88, queen $188.88, king $218.88. Also large selection of teenage bedroom sets. THE SECOND BEDROOM, 3451 El Cajon Blvd. Four blocks East of 805. Open 7 days. 280-0620; 280-5478.

Study the newspaper ad above to answer the following questions.

1. How much is the double bed?

   a. $48.88
   b. $98.88
   c. $148.88
   d. $188.88

2. What items are not for sale in this ad?

   a. beds
   b. sofas
   c. coffee tables
   d. lamps

3. Why are these items on sale?

   a. It's the end of the year.
   b. The business will close soon.
   c. The store just opened.
   d. It's a holiday weekend.

4. How much discount is being offered?

   a. $40 off
   b. Up to 50% off
   c. Up to 30% off
   d. $30 to $50 off

chapter 7

EMPLOYMENT: GETTING AND KEEPING A JOB

COMPETENCY OBJECTIVES

On completion of this unit the students will show orally, in writing, or through demonstration that they are able to use language needed in the following situations:

A. LOOKING FOR A JOB OR JOB TRAINING

- Use various sources to identify job training and employment opportunities.
- Interpret newspaper want ads related to employment.
- Use the telephone to inquire about job openings or training programs.
- Interpret and complete a job application form.
- Make an appointment for a job interview.

B. JOB INTERVIEW

- Ask questions concerning duties, hours, salary, qualifications, and fringe benefits.
- Answer questions concerning personal background, education, and experience, and state one's own strengths.
- Describe appropriate dress and behavior during a job interview.
- Make a follow-up call after an interview.

C. KEEPING A JOB

- Report work progress and completion of tasks.
- Initiate and respond to questions about personal interests, recreation, and hobbies.
- Report an absence from work.
- Ask for information as to the location of tools or equipment needed at the work site.
- Respond to a supervisor's criticism on the job.
- Inquire about and discuss job advancement opportunities and requirements.

NEEDS ASSESSMENT EXERCISE _____

EMPLOYMENT

I need to improve my English so that I can

_____ identify resources for job training.

_____ use newspapers and other resources to find job opportunities.

_____ use the telephone to inquire about jobs or job training.

_____ read and fill out an application for a job.

_____ make an appointment for a job interview.

_____ ask questions about duties, hours, salary, qualifications, and benefits in a job interview.

_____ answer questions about personal background, qualifications, education, and experience in a job interview.

_____ make a follow-up call after a job interview.

_____ report work progress and completion of job assignments to a supervisor or boss.

_____ talk with co-workers about recreation, sports, and interests.

_____ report an absence from work.

_____ ask for information about the location of tools or equipment needed at work.

_____ respond to a supervisor's criticism on the job.

_____ ask about and discuss a job promotion.

LOOKING FOR A JOB

A: You look tired. What have you been doing?
B: I've been looking for a job for two weeks now, but I can't find anything.
A: Did you check the want ads?
B: Yes, but they all say they need someone with experience.
A: What about the State Employment office? Have you gone there yet?
B: Yes, I went there and left an application, but they told me
   to come back in a week.
A: What are you going to do now?
B: I don't know. Do you have any ideas?

A: _____ .

Please Notice: The dialogue above is not finished. Talk with some other students and decide what could be said to finish it. Some ways to offer suggestions are:

Why don't you . . . .
If I were you, I would . . . .
I think you should . . . .
You might . . . .

PRACTICE

I've been looking for a job for two weeks now.
                            one month.
                    since last month.
                            Tuesday.
                            the beginning of the week.
                            I got here.

They told me to come back in a week.
                fill out an application.
                call them back.

They all say they need someone with experience.
                have enough applications.
                don't need anyone now.

INTERVIEW

1. Have you looked for a job in the United States before?
2. Where did you look?
   What did the people say?
   What did you do?
3. If you need a job here, where can you go?
4. In your country, how did people find jobs?
   Is it different here?
5. Are you looking for a job now?
   If yes, what kind?

LOOKING FOR JOB TRAINING

A: May I help you?
B: Yes. Do you have an electronic assembly training program?
A: What kind?
B: Electronic assembly.
A: Yes, we do. A new class begins next week.
B: Could you tell me how long it lasts?
A: Approximately six months.
B: Six months?
A: That's right.
B: Do I have to take any tests before enrolling?
A: Yes, you must pass an English test and a math test.
B: OK. How do I sign up for the tests?
A: Go down the hall to the Assessment Center.
   You can register there.
B: OK. Thanks for the information.

PRACTICE

Do you have an electronic assembly training program?
        auto mechanic
    a welding
    a computer
    a nurse assistant
    a clerical

Could you tell me how long it lasts?
        what the requirements are?
        how much it costs?
        how I can apply?
        when it starts?
        where I can register?

Practice calling to get information about job training. Use the cue words to help you form the questions.

    A: May I help you?
    B: (nurse assistant training program?)
    A: Yes, we do.
    B: (How long . . . last?)
    A: Six months.
    B: (When . . . begin?)
    A: On the first of the month.
    B: (tests?)
    A: Yes, you must pass an English test before you enroll.
    B: (How . . . register?)
    A: Come in to our office any day this week.
    B: Thank you.

INTERVIEW

1. Did you have a job in your country?
2. What kind of job would you like to have in the U.S.?
3. Have you had any job training in the U.S.?
4. Would you like to have job training here? What kind?
5. What do you think you need to do to prepare for this training?

Take-Home Assignment: Call a skills center, training school, or adult education office where training is offered. If you don't know the telephone number, look up the number in the yellow pages of the phone book. Ask about the training classes, write the information down and then report back to your class.

Types of Questions;

1. How long is the training?
2. When does it begin?
3. How do I apply?
4. What are the requirements?
5. How much is it?
6. What are the hours of the classes?

Reporting Back:

EXAMPLE: The office clerk said that the training was for six months.

1. CLERICAL. Type 45 wpm, knowledge of office methods, procedures, & equip. Ability to meet public. Good sal. fringe benefits. Apply Marine Corp. Exchange 10-2 MCRD Bldg. 16A

2. PART-TIME. Gardener's helper, no exper nec. $4.50 hr, own truck pref, 277-1702 aft. 6

3. NURSES' AIDES—exper. Days & PM's Carroll's Convalescent Hospital 622 So. Anza, El Cajon

4. NURSE'S AIDE
Weekends & on-call,
all shifts
Green Acres, 454-0344

5. COOKS wanted, must be capable of taking over kitchen. Apply in person Poway Mine Co. 1660-A Redding Rd., San Rivas

6. COOKS. Applications now being accepted for exper. cooks able to work day or nite shifts. Apply Hamburger House, 4060 Mesa Blvd. between 2:30 & 4:30. No phone calls please.

7. CLERICAL
FORD MOTOR CREDIT CO.
Desires an individual with a min. 2 yrs. finance company exp. for a clerical position. Excellent benefits. Contact Jim Cirks, 291-6650
An Equal Opportunity Employer M/F

Study the job ads above to answer the following questions.

1. If you would like to work in a restaurant, which ads should you look at?
   a. 1 and 5   b. 5 and 6   c. 2 and 6   d. 6 only

2. In which of the following ads do the jobs require experience?
   a. 3, 6, and 7   b. 2, 3, and 6   c. 1, 4, and 6   d. 3, 4, and 5

3. For which jobs must you apply in person?
   a. 1, 2, and 3   b. 1, 3, 5, and 6   c. 2, 3, 4, and 7   d. All of the ads

4. If you are looking for a job that provides health insurance, which ads would you be interested in?
   a. 5 and 6   b. 6 and 7   c. 1 and 7   d. None of them

AN APPOINTMENT FOR AN INTERVIEW

A: This is Personnel—may I help you?
B: Yes, I'd like to inquire about the job opening for a clerk typist.
A: Have you filed an application yet?
B: Yes, I was told to call today to make an appointment for an interview.
A: Your name, please.
B: Mary Green.
A: Would tomorrow at 10:00 be all right?
B: 10:00?
A: Yes, is that OK?
B: That's fine. Would you please tell me where you are located?
A: Downtown in the Financial Building at 5th and C, room 211.
B: What streets?
A: 5th and C.
B: Excuse me, whom should I ask for when I come in?
A: Just ask for the personnel manager at the front desk.
B: Thank you. I'll be there tomorrow at 10:00.

PRACTICE

I'd like to inquire about the job opening for a clerk typist.
    receptionist.
    mechanic.
    welder.

Would you please tell me where you are located?
    what I should bring with me?
    when I should call back?

Have you written the letter yet?   Yes, I wrote it last week.
    spoken to your boss
    given notice to your employer   _____ .
    seen the personnel manager

    _____ .

    _____ .

Pair Practice: Practice the conversation below with a partner. Use question words (Who? How much? Where? When? How long?) to request clarification of the underlined words.

EXAMPLE: Student A: Come tomorrow at <u>10:00</u> .
    Student B: What time?
    Student A: 10:00

1. Please ask for <u>Mr. Brown</u>.
2. Write a check for <u>$10.00</u>.
3. The training lasts <u>six months</u>.
4. Your appointment is <u>next Wednesday</u>.
5. Please come to <u>room 1221</u>.
6. Our office is on <u>Harrington Way</u>.

DUTIES, HOURS, SALARY, AND FRINGE BENEFITS _____

A: My job counselor informed me that you might have a job opening for a clerk typist. He told me to call you.
B: Yes, there could be an opening in a couple of weeks.
A: What are the qualifications for the job?
B: You have to type 55 words per minute.
A: Did you say 45 or 55 words per minute?
B: Fifty-five words per minute.
A: Is the job temporary or permanent, and what are the hours?
B: It's a permanent full-time job from 9 to 5, five days a week.
A: Can you tell me what the salary is?
B: The starting salary is $1200 including the basic fringe benefits such as health insurance, sick leave, and paid vacation.
A: $1200 a month?
B: Yes, that's right.
A: It sounds great. How can I apply for the job?
B: I can mail you an application, or you can pick one up in our personnel office.
A: Thank you for the information. I'll drop by today to pick one up.

PRACTICE

My job counselor informed me that you might have a job opening.
    told
    advised
    notified

He told me to call you.
    get in touch with you.
    fill out an application.
    make an appointment.

There could be an opening in a couple of weeks.
    a position available

Pair Practice: Practice the conversations below with a partner.

EXAMPLE: Student A: The hours are 8 to 3.
        Student B: Did you say 8 to 3?
        Student A: Yes, 8 to 3.

1. The salary is $950 a month.
2. There will be an opening in a couple of weeks.
3. The job is part-time—20 hours a week.
4. Benefits include sick leave and a two-week vacation after one year.
5. You must type 45 words per minute.

Pair Practice: Use the information on the chart to practice asking about job openings.

EXAMPLE: Student A: I'm calling about the job for a gardener. Is it permanent or temporary?
           Student B: It's temporary.
           Student A: Is it full-time or part-time?
           Student B: It's part-time.
           Student A: What are the hours?
           Student B: 9 to 5.
           (Continue)

I'm calling about the job for a . . .	Perm/ Temp	Full/ Part	Hours	Salary	Qualifications
Gardener	Temp	Part	Sat 9–5	$30/ day	Have own tools
Waiter	Perm	Full	3–11 Tues– Sun.	Min. Wage +tips	Speak Eng.
Assembler	Perm	Full	M–F 7–3	5.00/ hr.	Must know how to solder
Typist	Temp	Part	M–F 1–4	5.50/ hr.	Type 55 wpm

Take-Home Assignment: Look up some want ads in the newspaper and write the information about them in the chart below. If you don't have all the information, call the numbers in the ads and get the information. Bring the information back to class and share it.

Job	Perm/ Temp	Full/ Part	Hours	Salary	Qualifications
1.					
2.					
3.					
4.					

APPLYING FOR A JOB

Pair Practice: Practice the conversation below with your teacher and then with a partner. Use the cue words to help you form the questions and answers.

A: ABC Company. May I help you?
B: (Ask if the job for a clerk typist advertised in the paper is still open.)
A: Yes, the job is still open. We will accept applications until Friday.
B: (Ask about the qualifications.)
A: (Answer.)
B: (Ask about the hours.)
A: (Answer.)
B: (Ask about the salary and benefits.)
A: (Answer.)
B: (Ask if it is full-time or part-time.)
A: (Answer.)
B: (Ask how you can apply for the job.)
A: (Tell the person to come in and get an application and make an appointment for an interview.)

Study this picture and answer the questions below.

1. Who is the man in the picture?
2. What is he doing?
3. What are the women doing?
4. Describe the man.
5. Describe the woman in his office.
   What is she wearing?
   How does she look?
6. Describe the woman outside his office.
7. Who do you think will get the job? Why?
8. If you were the boss, who would you hire?
9. What do you think a person should wear to a job interview?

Group Exercise: Sit in groups of three or four and decide what a person should and shouldn't do on a job interview. Make a list of three things a person should do and three things a person shouldn't do. Then share your ideas with the rest of the class.

JOB INTERVIEW

Interviewer: How long have you lived in San Diego?
Applicant: I've lived in San Diego just a few months, but I've been in the U.S. since last year.
Interviewer: How much education have you had?
Applicant: I received my high school diploma in 1980 and have taken several clerical courses since then.
Interviewer: Have you worked in an office before?
Applicant: Yes, I worked as a clerk typist in San Francisco for six months.
Interviewer: When would you be available to start?
Applicant: I can start immediately.
Interviewer: OK, if you don't hear from us in a week, please give us a call.
Applicant: Thank you.

PRACTICE

I've taken several clerical courses since then.
        English
        math
        vocational

Have you worked in an office before?
        driven a truck
        operated a cash register
        managed a restaurant
        waited on tables
        taken dictation
        done mechanical work

When would you be available to start?
        take the job?

INTERVIEW

1. Have you ever had a job interview before?
   Where? When? For what job?
2. How did you feel during the interview?
3. What did the supervisor ask you during the interview?
4. What did you say?
5. Did you get the job?

SAMPLE INTERVIEW QUESTIONS

1. Do you have any experience in this type of work?
2. Why did you leave your last job? Did you like it?
3. What hours are you available for work?
4. Why do you think you would like to work for this company?
5. Are you looking for a temporary or a permanent job?
6. Why do you think you can handle this job?
7. What are your future career plans?
8. What salary do you expect?
9. Do you prefer working with others or by yourself?
10. How long did you work for your last employer?
11. What hobbies do you have?
12. Are you willing to work anywhere the company sends you?
13. Are you willing to work overtime?
14. Tell me about yourself. (This is the most difficult question to answer!)

Discuss the following questions you might want to ask an employer or personnel manager:

1. Do you have medical coverage or workers' compensation? Does it cover anyone else in my family?
2. How much vacation time and/or sick leave do I earn each year?
3. What is the starting salary?
4. What are the hours of the job?
5. What are the duties of the job?
6. What are the opportunities for promotion?

JOB INTERVIEW

Pair Practice: Ask each other the following questions.

1. How long have you lived in _____ ?
2. How much education have you had?
3. What type of work would you like to do?
4. Do you have any experience in this type of work?
5. Are you looking for temporary or permanent work?
6. What hours are you available to work?
7. Why do you think you can handle this job?
8. What are your future plans?
9. When would you be available to start?
10. Are you willing to work overtime?

Student A: Ask student B the questions on the left.
Student B: Choose the correct response from the right-hand column.

Student A
1. Do you have any experience in this type of work?
2. What are your future career plans?
3. Why did you leave your last job?
4. What are your strengths?
5. What salary do you expect?
6. Do you want full-time or part-time work?

Student B
1. I would like to become a nurse assistant.
2. The entry level wage with the opportunity to advance.
3. I would prefer full-time, but I can work part-time if that is all that is open.
4. I was laid off because it was a temporary assignment.
5. Yes. I worked as a home health aide for six months.
6. I am reliable and I work hard. On my last job, I only missed one day of work.

Interviewing for a Job

Discuss each of the following interview questions and answers with another student. Decide what is wrong with each answer. Can you think of a better answer?

a. What experience do you have in this type of work?
   Answer: Oh, I can do anything. Give me a chance.

   Better answer: _____

b. How did you like your last job and employer?
   Answer: My employer was impossible to work for. That's why I quit.

   Better answer: _____

c. What salary do you expect?
   Answer: I expect at least $600.

   Better answer: _____

d. Are you looking for permanent employment?
   Answer: I just want a summer job. I'm moving out of town in September.

   Better answer: _____

e. Why have you been out of work for a year?
   Answer: I just didn't feel like working.

   Better answer: _____

f. Why do you think you would like to work for this company?
   Answer: Because the pay is good.

   Better answer: _____

FOLLOW-UP CALL AFTER AN INTERVIEW _____

A: I'm calling to inquire about the status of my application
for the position of clerk typist.
B: Have you had an interview yet?
A: Yes, I was interviewed three days ago and I haven't heard
anything. The secretary said she would call me.
B: What is your name?
A: Lee Smith.
B: I'm sorry. That position has been filled. We may have
additional openings next month.

PRACTICE

Have you had an interview yet?
      taken the test
      made an appointment
      sent in your application

I was interviewed three days ago.
      hired
      promoted
      given a raise

The secretary said she would call me.
      let me know.
      notify me.
      file my application.
      tell the boss.

FILLING OUT EMPLOYMENT APPLICATIONS

Discuss this application for employment with your teacher. Then fill out the application for yourself.

_____ Application for Employment

1. Title of position _____ Beginning date _____ Salary _____
    Mr.
2. Name Mrs. _____
    Miss   Last (Print)   First   Middle   (Maiden name)
3. Mailing address _____ Home telephone _____
                    Street and No.   City   State   Zip code Alternate no. _____
4. How long immediately preceding this date have you lived in this county? _____
5. In case of accident, notify _____ Address _____ Phone _____
                                                                        U.S.
6. Age _____ Date of birth _____ Social Security no. ____ / ____ / ____ Citizen? _____
7. Marital Status: Single _____ Married _____ Widowed _____ Separated _____ Divorced ___
8. If married, spouse is employed by: _____ City _____
9. List ages and relationship of all persons dependent on you _____

    _____
10. Indicate any disease or physical disability, defect, or infirmity _____
    Indicate nature and extent of handicap, whether permanent, and whether military service-connected

    _____
11. Circle the highest grade you
    completed in each school   Name and location of school   Dates

    High School 9 10 11 12   Course
    _____
    College   1   2   3   4   Major   Minors
    _____
    Post-grad: Course
    Semester hrs. _____ _____
    _____
    Professional/vocational schools   Courses (if part-
                                                                 time, indicate)
    _____

12. Give your complete employment record during the last five years, and ALSO any earlier experience
    of the kind required for this kind of position. List your positions in the order of dates, your present
    or most recent position first.

From Mo./Yr.	To Mo./Yr.	Employer's name, address, telephone number, and name of last supervisor	Salary	Position—state your title, describe duties	Reason for leaving

13. What are your hobbies and interests? _____

    _____
14. Applicant's signature _____ Date _____

COFFEE BREAK/SMALL TALK ON THE JOB

A: Hi. I'm _____ . Are you new here?
B: Yes. I just started two weeks ago.
A: How do you like it so far?
B: I like it, but there is a lot to learn.
A: Don't worry. You'll get used to it. How about a cup of coffee?
B: Thanks. I'd like one. How long have you been here?
A: Two years. It's a nice day today, isn't it?
B: Yes. It's too bad we have to stay indoors.
A: You know what? It's already time to go back to work.
  Nice to talk to you.
B: Yes. Thanks for the coffee. Maybe I'll see you later.

Conversation Openers:

Do you have the time?
Do you work in this department?
Do I know you?
It's a nice day, isn't it?
Did you hear about. . .?
How long have you been here?
You look nice today.
That's a nice jacket.
Did you see the game last night?

Pair Practice: Choose a conversation opener question from the list above and ask another student the question. Ask another question to respond to his or her answer to keep the conversation going.

EXAMPLE: Student A: Do you work in this department?
               Student B: Yes, I do.
               Student A: Really? How long have you been here?

A: Did you watch the game last night?
B: No, I missed it. What was the score?
A: It was really close. In the last minute, our team won—7 to 6.
B: You're kidding. I wish I'd seen it. Do you ever play soccer?
A: I used to play all the time, but I haven't lately. How about you?

B: _____ .

PRACTICE

Do you ever play soccer?
     football?
     baseball?
     tennis?
     golf?

Do you ever go swimming?
     fishing?
     jogging?
     skiing?
     camping?
     biking?
     diving?

I used to play soccer.
   sing.
   dance.
   play the violin.

INTERVIEW

Ask your partner the following questions. Write down the answers so that you can share them with the rest of the class.

1. Did you play a sport in your country? Which one?
2. Did you like to watch a sport in your country? Which one?
3. Do you ever play a sport in the U.S.? Which one? How often do you play?
4. Do you watch sports in person or on TV now?
   What is your favorite sport to watch?
5. What was the last game that you watched?
   Who won? What was the score?

CALLING IN SICK

A: ABC Company.
B: May I speak to my supervisor, John Miller?
A: He's not in yet. May I take a message?

B: Yes, this is _____ .
   Would you please tell him that I can't come to work today because I've got the flu?
A: What shift do you work?
B: 3 to 11.
A: OK, I'll give him the message.

PRACTICE

I can't come to work because I've got the flu.
                              a high fever.
                              a personal emergency.
                              a sick child.

Would you please tell him that I can't come to work?
Could
Can
Will

INTERVIEW

1. Do you work? Have you ever worked in the U.S.?
2. When you worked, what did you do when you were sick?
3. What was the policy about reporting an absence from work?
4. In your country, if you couldn't go to work, what did you do? Was the policy different from in the U.S.?
5. In the United States what are some acceptable reasons for being absent from work?

REPORTING WORK PROGRESS

    A: How are you doing?
    B: OK. I set up the back room for 12 people and
        made all the salads for lunch tomorrow.
    A: Have you filled the salt and pepper shakers yet?
    B: No, but I'll get it done before I leave today.
    A: Don't forget to punch your time card before you leave.
    B: I won't.

Pair Practice: Practice the conversation below with your class, substituting items 1–5 for the underlined words. Then sit in pairs and practice with a partner. Can you think of new substitutions?

EXAMPLE: (sign out—leave)
            Student A: Don't forget to <u>sign out</u> before
                         you <u>leave</u>.
            Student B: I won't.

1. lock the door—leave
2. close the windows—leave
3. open the windows—spray
4. clean the floors—wash the windows
5. see the boss—go

Pair Practice: Look at the pictures on the next page. Practice the following conversation with your class and then with a partner.

EXAMPLE: (wash the dishes—empty the trash)
            Student A: After you wash the dishes, be sure to empty the trash.
            Student B: OK, I will.

1. wash the dishes—empty the trash.
2. fill the gas tank—check the oil
3. fill out the form—take it to the clerk
4. close the lid—press the start button
5. spray the cabinets—leave the room
6. stock the shelves—lock the cabinets
7. plug in the machine—flip on the switch
8. insert the disk—turn on the power

Pair Practice: Use the following conversation to ask how to find the tools listed below the conversation. Write in the name of the tool when you find the correct location. Practice using formal and informal ways to ask for something.

A: Can you tell me where I can find the _____ ?

B: In the tool shed.

A: I've already looked. Where in the tool shed?

B: On the _____ shelf _____ .

(bolts, saw, flashlight, screwdriver)

Formal: Can you tell me where I can find the _____ ?

Where can I find the _____ ?

Informal: Where's the _____ ?

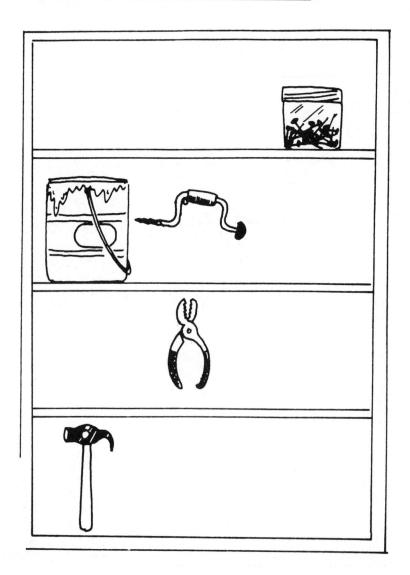

LOCATING TOOLS—STUDENT B

Pair Practice: Use the following conversation to ask how to find the tools listed below the conversation. Write in the name of the tool when you find the correct location. Practice using formal and informal ways to ask for something.

A: Can you tell me where I can find the _____ ?
B: In the tool shed.
A: I've already looked. Where in the tool shed?

B: On the _____ shelf _____ .

(nails, can of paint, pliers, hammer)

Formal: Can you tell me where I can find the _____ ?

Where can I find the _____ ?

Informal: Where's the _____ ?

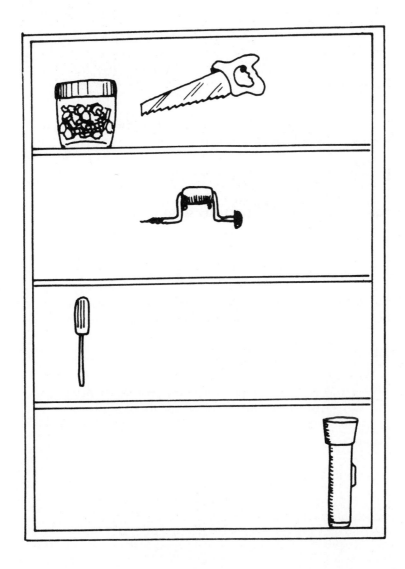

Discuss each of the following boss's comments and employee responses. Decide what is wrong with each employee response. Can you think of a better response?

1. Boss: Jack, we've got 10 customers in line. Hurry it up. Can't you work faster?
    Employee: It's not my fault. This lady has changed her order three times.

    Better Answer: _____

2. Boss: This paint job is really sloppy. You've got to be more careful.
    Employee: It's Joe's fault. He told me to hurry up.

    Better Answer: _____

3. Boss: You're not listening. I told you to get 50 towels, not 15.
    Employee: You're wrong about that. I heard you say 15.

    Better Answer: _____

4. Boss: This is wrong. You didn't do it correctly.
    Employee: Well, nobody explained it to me.

    Better Answer: _____

5. Boss: You're making too many mistakes. Keep your mind on the job.
    Employee: I can't help it. I just broke up with my girlfriend.

    Better Answer: _____

6. Boss: If you're late one more time, you're out of here.
    Employee: But I couldn't help it. My car broke down.

    Better Answer: _____

ASKING FOR A PROMOTION

A: Hi, How's it going?
B: All right. I'm on a break. If you've got a minute, may I ask you a question?
A: Sure.
B: You know, I've been here 10 months now and I was just wondering what the possibilities might be for a promotion or a raise?
A: Well, you must have worked here for at least a year and have had no poor performance reviews.
B: I think I will qualify in a couple of months. What do I have to do to be considered?
A: Let me think about it. I'll talk to your supervisor. If nothing else, you should get an automatic pay increase after one year.
B: Thanks. I enjoy working here. If I can move up here, I'd like to stay.

PRACTICE

I was just wondering what the possibilities are for a promotion?

raise.
transfer.
bonus.
job change.

If I can move up, I'd like to stay.
    get a promotion
    get a transfer
    improve my skills
    get a raise

INTERVIEW

1. Have you ever gotten a raise on a job in the U.S.? If yes, how did you get it?
2. In your country, how do people get raises?
3. Are raises automatic in some jobs?

1. What do you think he used to do in his country?
When did this interview take place?
What do you think he was saying to the personnel manager?

2. What kinds of jobs do you think the personnel manager offered him?
Why?

3. Which job did he take?
What did he do while he was working as a stock clerk?
Why?

4. What kind of job does he have now?
What did he use to do?
What do you think he is telling the new stock clerk?

INTERVIEW

What did you use to do in your country?
What would you like to do in the U.S.?

Pair Practice: Sit with another student. Complete the sentences below, and then share your answers with the class.

EXAMPLE: If <u>Ann</u> wants to be a <u>welder</u>, she should <u>take a welding class</u>.

1. **a.** If _____ wants to be a _____ , he/she should

   _____ .

   b. he/she could _____ .

   c. he/she might _____ .

2. **a.** If _____ takes an entry level job first, he/she

   will _____ .

   b. he/she could _____ .

   c. he/she might _____ .

3. **a.** If _____ studies _____ , he/she will _____

   _____ .

   b. he/she should _____ .

   c. he/she might _____ .

chapter 8

COMMUNITY RESOURCES

COMPETENCY OBJECTIVES

On completion of this unit the students will show orally, in writing, or through demonstration that they are able to use language needed in the following situations:

A. POSTAL SERVICES

- Ask and respond to questions regarding tracing lost mail.
- Ask and respond to questions regarding insuring and registering mail.
- Interpret written information to determine correct postage.
- Interpret postal service forms for mailing a package outside the country.

B. COMMUNICATION WITH SCHOOLS

- Obtain information about day care centers.
- Interpret a newspaper ad for a day care center.
- Initiate and respond appropriately to oral communication with a child's teacher.

C. RECREATION AND ENTERTAINMENT

- Ask about and describe places of interest in the U.S. and one's native country.
- Interpret a TV program schedule.
- Interpret movie ads in a newspaper.
- Use the index in the newspaper to locate information.

D. COMMUNITY SERVICES

- Use the telephone book to locate and access community resources which provide specific problem-solving assistance.
- Ask and respond to questions regarding the use of the public library.
- Interpret information from a weather forecast.

NEEDS ASSESSMENT EXERCISE

COMMUNITY RESOURCES

I need to improve my English so that I can

_____ ask and answer questions about tracing lost mail.

_____ ask and answer questions about insuring and registering mail.

_____ read and understand information about postage rates.

_____ read and fill out postal service forms to mail a package outside the country.

_____ use newspaper ads and other resources to get information about day care centers.

_____ communicate with my children's school teachers.

_____ ask about and describe places of interest in the U.S. and my native country.

_____ read and understand a TV program schedule.

_____ read and understand movie ads in the newspaper.

_____ use the index in a newspaper to locate information.

_____ use the telephone book to locate community resources which can provide specific problem-solving assistance.

_____ ask and respond to questions about services in a public library.

_____ understand and use information from a weather forecast.

TRACING A LOST PACKAGE

A: I sent a package to my mother in the Philippines a month ago, and she hasn't received it yet.
B: It should have gotten there by now. Did you insure it?
A: No, I didn't. Would it be possible for you to put a tracer on it?
B: We can try, but I can't guarantee anything. You should have insured it.
A: I guess I should have insured it. But I took it for granted it would get there.
B: Just fill out this form, please.

PRACTICE

You should have insured it.
     registered it.
     sent it airmail.
     sent it special delivery.
     put more stamps on it.
     put a return address on it.

Would it be possible for you to put a tracer on it?
         give me a receipt?
         stop delivery?
         change the name on my post office box?

INTERVIEW

Have you ever lost anything in the mail?
If yes, what was it?
Where were you sending it?
Did you report it to the post office?
What happened?

SHOULD I REGISTER OR INSURE?

A: I want to send my aunt in Detroit $100 in cash, and I want to make sure it gets there. How should I send it?

B: If you are sending money, you should register it. It's the safest way.

A: What's the difference between registering and insuring mail?

B: Money and negotiable items must be registered, and each carrier must sign for it. If you insure something that gets lost, you will be reimbursed.

A: How much would it cost to register $100?

B: The rates have gone up again. It would cost $4.50.

A: That's a lot. But to play it safe, I guess I'd better do that. How long will it take for the money to get to Detroit?

B: It should be delivered by Monday.

PRACTICE

What is the difference between registering and insuring?
         first class and second class?
         express mail and first class?

Money must be registered.
Negotiable items

You will be reimbursed.
         given a receipt.
         paid back.
         notified.

It should be returned.
         stamped.
         sealed.
         taped.
         registered.
         insured.

How long will it take for the money to get to Detroit?
         the package to get there?
         to get the money back?

READING POSTAL INFORMATION CHARTS

Student A: Student B will ask you questions. Listen to the questions carefully. If you don't understand a question, ask student B to repeat it. Look at the chart below to find the information you need to answer each question. When you finish, check your answers together, and then compare them with those of the rest of the class.

SPECIAL SERVICES—DOMESTIC MAIL ONLY

INSURANCE
For Coverage Against Loss or Damage

Fees (in addition to postage)

Liability	Fee
$ 0.01 to $ 50.00	$0.70
50.01 to 100.00	1.50
100.01 to 150.00	1.90
150.01 to 200.00	2.20
200.01 to 300.00	3.15
300.01 to 400.00	4.30
400.01 to 500.00	5.00

REGISTRY
For Maximum Protection and Security

Value	Fees in addition to postage	
	For articles covered by Postal Insurance	For articles not covered by Postal Insurance
$0.01 to 100.00	$4.50	$4.40
$100.01 to 500.00 500.01 to 1,000.00 For higher values, consult Postmaster	4.85 5.25	4.70 5.05

Now, ask student B the following questions. Student B will get the answers from the chart on the next page. After you have compared your answers together, compare them with those of the rest of the class.

1. If a letter weighs 2 ounces, how much will it cost to mail it first class?
   _____

2. If I have a letter that weighs 3 1/2 ounces, how much will it cost to mail it first class? _____

3. How much would it cost me to send a 5-ounce letter by express mail?
   _____

4. If I need to send a letter by express mail, when will it arrive? _____
   _____

5. How much would it cost to send a 1-pound package by express mail?
   _____

6. If it costs $2.25 to mail an 11-ounce letter, how much would it cost to send a 12-ounce letter? _____

7. Have you ever mailed anything by express mail?

Student B: Ask student A the following questions. Student A will get the answers from the chart on the previous page. After you have finished, compare your answers together. Then compare them with those of the rest of the class.

1. How much would it cost to insure a package worth $22? _____

2. How much would it cost to insure a $300 camera? _____

3. How much would it cost to register an insured gift worth $75? _____

    _____

4. How much would it cost to register a check for $700 that is not insured?

    _____

5. Is it more expensive to register or insure mail? _____

6. Does the insurance fee cover the postage also? _____

7. Have you ever insured something you have sent in the mail? What?

Now, student A will ask you some questions. Listen to the questions carefully. If you don't understand a question, ask student A to repeat it. Look at the chart below to find the information you need to answer each question. When you finish, check your answers together, and then compare them with those of the rest of the class.

POSTAGE RATES

NEXT DAY SERVICE

AN OVERNIGHT DELIVERY SERVICE THAT'S FAST, RELIABLE, CONVENIENT AND ECONOMICAL

Express Mail Service is available 7 days a week, 365 days a year (at no additional charge) for mailable items up to 70 pounds in weight and 108 inches in combined length and girth.

Flat rates for Post Office to Addressee service: letter rate (up to 8 ounces), $8.75; up to 2 lbs., $12.00; over 2 lbs. and up to 5 lbs., $15.25; consult Postmaster for rates for items exceeding 5 lbs. up to 70 lbs.

FIRST-CLASS

LETTER RATES:

1st ounce... $0.25
Each additional ounce... 0.20

For pieces not exceeding (oz.)	The Rate Is	For pieces not exceeding (oz.)	The Rate Is
1	$0.25	7	$1.45
2	0.45	8	1.65
3	0.65	9	1.85
4	0.85	10	2.05
5	1.05	11	2.25
6	1.25		

MAILING A PACKAGE OUTSIDE THE COUNTRY

United States Postal Service	No.

FROM Expéditeur

John Brown
5345 University Ave
Los Angeles, CA
90025

Sender's Instructions
If parcel is undeliverable:

Dispositions de l'expéditeur
En cas de non-livraison

☒ **Return to sender**
Renvoyer à l'origine
(NOTE: Parcel will be returned by surface and at sender's expense.)

☐ **Forward to:** Réexpédié à

TO Destinataire

Maria Lopez
54361 Avenida Azul
Mexico City,
Mexico

☐ **Abandon**   Abandonné

QTY.	Itemized List of Contents Please Print	VALUE (US $)
2	men's shirts	85.00
1	pair of pants	16.00
2	women's sweaters	50.00
2	skirts	45.00

Signature of Sender *John Brown*	Date 6-10-90

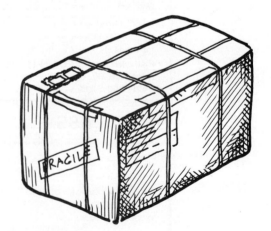

Study the form above to answer the following questions.

1. Who will receive the package?
2. Who is sending the package?
3. How many shirts are being sent?
4. How much are the shirts worth?
5. If the package cannot be delivered because the person has moved, what will happen to the package?

Look at the following questions. Each set of questions goes with one of the pictures above. Discuss the questions with a partner, and then share your answers with the rest of the class. Next, write a story to go with the pictures.

1. What did he do before he went to the post office?
   What did he do after he got to the post office?
2. What happened after he mailed the package?
   What did she do after she opened the package?
3. What did she do when she got to the post office?
   What do you think the clerk did when she saw the broken plate?
4. What did the post office do after she filed an insurance claim?

INTERVIEW

1. Has the post office ever lost or damaged anything you have mailed?
   What did you do?
2. Have you ever filed a claim for insured mail that has been lost or damaged?

   registered
   COD
   Express

   What was the result?

PRESCHOOL PROGRAM

Mon.-Thurs. 7:30 am-6:30 pm
Fri. 7:30 am-Midnight
Sat. 5:00 pm-Midnight

**For Registration and
Space Reservation - Please Call:
555-5566**

NEW PRESCHOOL PROGRAM
- Full/Half Day Programs
- Ages 2-5 (toilet training available)
- Cognitive Skills, Self-Image Development, Physical Fitness
- Large Playground
- Snacks

DROP-IN DAY CARE
- State Licensed
- Ages 6 mos. and up
- Infant Developmental Play Activities
- CPR Trained
- Weekend Evenings til Midnight

A: ABC Day Care Center.
B: Hello. I would like some information about your day care center.
A: Just a minute. I'll connect you with our director.
C: May I help you?
A: Yes. I am interested in enrolling my son in a day care center. May I ask you a few questions?
C: Certainly.
A: How old must a child be to attend?
C: We accept children two to five years old. Two-year-olds should be toilet trained before they come.
A: What are your hours?
C: 7:30 A.M. to 6:30 P.M.
A: How much do you charge?
C: We have both full-day and half-day care plans. The tuition for five full days would be $270, and the half-day tuition is $200.
A: Does the tuition include lunch?
B: No. Children are expected to bring their own lunches. We provide two snacks per day.
A: Would it be possible to visit your center?
B: Yes. Just notify us a day ahead so that we can schedule your visit.
A: Thank you for the information.

PRACTICE

I am interested in enrolling my child in a day care center.
preschool.
an extended care program.

How much do you charge?
is the tuition?
are the fees?

Does the tuition include lunch?
snacks?
activity fees?

Children are expected to bring their own lunches.
bring a change of clothes.
have their immunizations updated.
take naps.

OTHER IMPORTANT QUESTIONS:

What are your hours?
How long are you open?
Are you open year round?
Are you open on holidays?
Do you have any openings?
a waiting list?
How do I register?

What qualifications do your teachers have?
What is your policy regarding discipline/punishment?
illness?
naps?
religious holidays?
snacks?
dress?
visits by parents?

Pair Practice: Sit in pairs and practice calling to get information about a day care center. Use words below to help you form the questions and answers.

Student A.
1. Information?
2. Ages?
3. Hours?
4. Tuition?

5. Lunch?
6. Qualifications—teachers?

7. Number of children per teacher?
8. Policy—illness?

9. Openings?

10. Possible to visit?

Student B.
1. Certainly
2. Two to five years old
3. 7:00 A.M. to 6:00 P.M.
4. $275—full day
   $200—half day
5. No—only snacks
6. Degree in child development

7. Six children per teacher

8. If child has a fever, constant cough, upset stomach, rash, or infected sores, he or she must stay home.
9. A few—depends on the age

10. Yes, by appointment

Take-Home Assignment: Call two day care centers or preschools in your area and ask questions to get the following information. Write the information in the chart below and bring it to class to share with the other students.

1	Minimum age	Hours	Fees—FT	Fees—PT	Lunch?
2					

A: Hello. I am _____ 's mother (father).
How is he doing?
B: He's doing fine, except in math.
A: Oh, really? What's the problem?
B: His grades have dropped because he hasn't been doing his homework regularly.
A: Thanks for telling me. I will make sure that he does his homework from now on.

PRACTICE

He's doing fine, except in math.
                        spelling.
                        English.
                        physical education.
                        handwriting.
                        art.
                        social studies.

I will make sure that he does his homework.
                        gets glasses.
                        comes to school on time.
                        studies for the tests.
                        returns the book.

Problems:

He doesn't pay attention.
He doesn't participate in class.
He doesn't do his homework.
He has poor study habits.
He doesn't try hard enough.
He fools around too much.
He has excessive tardiness.

Compliments:

He is improving.
He tries hard.
He pays attention.
He is well behaved.
He shows sincere effort.
He has good study habits.
He sets a good example.

Pair Practice: Practice the conversation below substituting the listed words for the underlined words in the dialogue. Practice with your class first and then with a partner.

EXAMPLE: 1. Ann's mother
          2. English
          3. doesn't participate in class

    Student A: Hello. I'm <u>Ann's mother</u>.
                               1
                    How is she doing?
    Student B: She's doing fine, except in <u>English</u>.
    Student A: What's the problem?   2
    Student B: She <u>doesn't participate in class</u>.
                              3
    Student A: Thanks for telling me. I will make sure she
                    <u>participates in class from now on</u>.
                                3

1. John's father
2. math
3. doesn't do his homework

1. Sue's mother
2. social studies
3. has been late to class six times

1. Jim's father
2. reading
3. has trouble seeing the blackboard

1. Lee's mother
2. spelling
3. doesn't practice her new spelling words

LIBRARY

A: May I help you?
B: Yes, I'd like to get a library card.
A: OK, I need some ID with your current address on it.
B: Is my rent receipt OK?
A: Yes, that's fine.
B: How many books can I check out at one time?
A: No more than six.
B: And when do I have to bring back the books?
A: In one month.
   The due date is in the front of the book.
B: Oh, I see. They're due on the tenth.
A: Don't be late. If you bring them back late, you'll be
   charged a fine.

PRACTICE

When do I have to bring back the books?
                 turn in the papers?
                 fill out the forms?

Bring them back _____ .

Turn them in _____ .

Fill them out _____ .

Can I check out the book?   Yes, you can check it out.

   take off the book cover?   Yes, you can _____ .

   wipe off the table?   Yes, you can _____ .

INTERVIEW

1. Have you ever been to the library in the city where you live now?
2. Did you go to a library in your country?
3. If you could check out any book from the library, what kind of book would
   you be interested in?

Take-Home Assignment: Go to the library near your home, or call the library. Find out
the days and hours the library is open. Then make a list of several things you can check
out of the library. Bring your information to class and share it with the other students.

WEATHER FORECAST

A: How about going to the beach for a picnic this weekend?
B: That sounds great, but what about the weather?
A: Just a minute, I'll call to get the forecast.
B: According to the forecast, it should be nice—cloudy in the morning and sunny in the afternoon.
A: What about the temperature?
B: It said 70s along the coast and about 80 degrees inland.
A: Let's hope that's right. I don't always trust the forecast. Although the weather forecaster says it will be nice, it may rain.
B: We'll just have to take our chances.

PRACTICE

How about going to the beach for a picnic?
         park
         mountains
         river
         lake

It should be nice.
     beautiful.
     warm.
     hazy.
     smoggy.
     foggy.
     sunny in the afternoon.
     hot.
     cold.
     muggy.
     humid.

Although the weather forecaster says it will be nice, it may rain.
Even though
                          sprinkle.
                 might pour.
                    snow.
              could be cloudy.
                   foggy.
                   chilly.
                   freezing.

What do you do when it rains?
                  snows?

What do you do when it's sunny?
                  chilly?
                  freezing?

PRACTICE

Practice talking with your classmates about going to each of the places pictured above. Then practice with a partner. Use the sentences below to start your conversations.

How about going _____ this weekend?

Would you like to go _____ ?

Do you want to go _____ ?

Let's go _____ .

Pair Practice: (Two people from different countries, if possible). Discuss the questions below with your partner. Then share your answers with the rest of the class.

Student A: If I came to your country, what would you take me to see?

Student B: I would take you to _____ .
Student A: Why? What could I do there?
                         What could I see there?

List the interesting places to visit in the city where you live now.

1. _____

2. _____

3. _____

4. _____

5. _____

Find someone who has been to each place. Then ask one question about the place. Talk with your teacher about other questions you could ask.

EXAMPLE: Student A: Have you ever been to Disneyland?
                    Student B: Yes, I have.
                    Student A: How much does it cost to go in?
                    Student B: (Answer the question.)

READING A PROGRAM GUIDE

Tonight, July 30

Ch.	6:00	6:30	7:00	7:30	8:00	8:30	9:00	9:30	10:00	10:30
2	CBS News	News	Star Search		Kate & Allie	Frank's Place	Tour Of Duty		West 57th	
4	Fight Back!	Mama's Family	It's A Living	The Sheriff	Facts of Life	227	Golden Girls	Amen	Hunter	
5	Movie: "Stick"				Movie: "Murphy's Law"				News	Sportspage
6	Stark Trek		Star Trek: The Next Generation		Reporters		Dirty Dozen: The Series		Friday The 13th: The Series	
7	News	ABC News	D.C. Follies	Hollywood	Supercarrier		Ohara		Hotel	
8	CBS News	News	Fight Back!	Public Affairs	Kate & Allie	Frank's Place	Tour of Duty		West 57th	
9	T.J. Hooker		Hardcastle and McCormick		Miss California-USA Pageant				Movie: "Sessions"	
10	D.C. Follies	The Sheriff	Big Spin	Win Lose	Supercarrier		Ohara		Hotel	
11	Small Wonder	Facts of Life	Big Spin	Family Ties	Reporters		Dirty Dozen: The Series		News	9 to 5
12	Sabado Gigante							Deportivos	Boxeo Desde Mexico	

Study the TV schedule above to answer the following questions.

1. What channels show the news at 6:00 P.M.?

   a. 2, 7, 8
   b. 4, 10
   c. 6, 8, 10
   d. 2, 8

2. How long does the CBS news at 6:00 last?

   a. 1 hour
   b. 1/2 hour
   c. 1 1/2 hours
   d. 2 hours

3. What comes on after the "Big Spin" on channel 10?

   a. "The Sheriff"
   b. "Family Ties"
   c. "Win Lose"
   d. "Facts of Life"

4. What channel is the movie Murphy's Law on?

   a. 6
   b. 4
   c. 9
   d. 5

5. What comes on before the news at 11:00 on channel 7?

   a. "West 57th St."
   b. "Hotel"
   c. "Hunter"
   d. a movie

GANN THEATRES

$3⁵⁰ BARGAIN TODAY
FOR PERFORMANCES
IN (PARENTHESIS)

ADVANCE TICKETS AVAILABLE
THROUGHOUT THE DAY FOR
ALL OF TODAY'S PERFORMANCES

★ PRESENTED IN **STEREO** WHERE NOTED ★

OCEANSIDE 8
EL CAMINO REAL
439-7008   AT HWY 78

DEAD POOL
(12:00)-2:15-4:30-7:00-9:30 (R) ★

CROCODILE DUNDEE II
(12:00)-2:30-5:00-7:30-10:00 (PG)

TOM CRUISE
COCKTAIL
(11:30)-2:00-4:30-7:15-10:00 (R)
SORRY, NO PASSES

CADDYSHACK II
7:30-9:30 (PG) ★

BULL DURHAM
(11:45)-2:15-4:45-7:15-9:45 (R)

JAMIE LEE CURTIS
A FISH CALLED WANDA
(11:45)-2:15-4:45-7:15-9:45 (R)
SORRY, NO PASSES

MIDNIGHT RUN
(11:30)-2:00-4:30-7:15-10:00 (R)

UNIV. TOWNE CTR. 6
4525 LA JOLLA
452-7766   VILLAGE DR.

COMING TO AMERICA
(11:30)-1:45-4:15-7:00-9:30 (R)

A FISH CALLED WANDA
(11:45)-2:00-4:30-7:15-9:45 (R)
SORRY, NO PASSES

MIDNIGHT RUN
(11:30)-2:00-4:30-7:15-10:00 (R) ★

ARTHUR 2
(12:15)-4:40-9:00 (PG)
CADDYSHACK 2
2:30-7:00 (PG)

BULL DURHAM
7:30-9:45 (R)

**THE NEW ADVENTURES OF
PIPPI LONGSTOCKING**
(12:00)-2:15-4:45 (G)

DEAD POOL
(12:00)-2:15-4:45-7:40-10:00 (R) ★

PLAZA BONITA 6
PLAZA BONITA CIR.
479-6266   NATL CITY

CROCODILE DUNDEE II
(11:30)-2:15-5:00-7:45-10:15 (PG)

MICHAEL McKEAN
SHORT CIRCUIT 2
(11:30)-2:00-4:30-7:15-10:00 (PG)

JOHN CLEESE
A FISH CALLED WANDA
(11:15)-2:00-4:45-7:30-10:15 (R)
SORRY, NO PASSES

WALT DISNEY'S
BAMBI
(11:30)-1:45-4:00-6:15-8:30 (G)

CLINT EASTWOOD
DEAD POOL
(12:00)-2:30-5:00-7:30-10:15 (R) ★

**THE NEW ADVENTURES OF
PIPPI LONGSTOCKING**
(12:00)-2:45-5:30 (G)

BULL DURHAM
8:00-10:15 (R)

SPORTS ARENA 6
3350 SPORTS
223-5333   ARENA BLVD.

**THE NEW ADVENTURES OF
PIPPI LONGSTOCKING**
(11:15)-1:15-3:15-5:30 (G)

BULL DURHAM
7:30-10:00 (R)

WALT DISNEY'S
BAMBI
(12:00)-2:00-3:45-5:30-7:00 (G)

ARTHUR 2
9:30 p.m. (PG)

CROCODILE DUNDEE II
(11:45)-2:15-4:45-7:15-9:45 (PG)

COMING TO AMERICA
(11:30)-2:00-4:30-7:15-10:00 (R) ★

BIG TOP PEE WEE
(11:45)-2:30-4:45-7:00-9:15 (PG)

CLINT EASTWOOD
DEAD POOL
(12:15)-2:30-5:00-7:30-9:45 (R) ★

Study the movie ad above to answer the following questions.

1. How many theaters are showing the movie *Bambi*?
2. If you were taking small children to a movie in the Sports Arena, which ones would be most appropriate according to the ratings?
3. If you went to see *Coming to America* at the University Town Center, what time would you get a bargain rate?
4. What is the latest time you could see *Midnight Run* at any theater?
5. According to the ratings, which movie would be more appropriate for a teenager—*Coming to America* or *Crocodile Dundee II*?

```
┌─────────────────────────────────┐
│            INDEX                │
│                                 │
│          116 pages              │
│                                 │
│  Bridge                E-3      │
│  Classified Ads        E-7-20   │
│  Comics                C-12     │
│  Crossword             E-9      │
│  Editorials            B-10     │
│  Entertainment/Movies  D-7, 8   │
│  Financial             A-21-28  │
│  Horoscope             A-11     │
│  Jumble                E-4      │
│  Ann Landers           D-2      │
│  Obituaries            B-4      │
│  Scrabble              E-6      │
│  Sports                C-1      │
│  Television            D-5, 6   │
│  Weather               E-6      │
└─────────────────────────────────┘
```

Study the newspaper index above to find the answer to the following questions.

1. What page can you find the movie ads on?

   a. D-7
   b. D-6
   c. D-5
   d. A-11

2. What section should you look in to find the latest baseball scores?

   a. Editorials
   b. Sports
   c. Entertainment
   d. Crossword

3. What page should you turn to to look for a job ad?

   a. B-10
   b. D-7, 8
   c. E-7–20
   d. A-21–28

4. Where can you find the funny cartoons?

   a. E-9
   b. E-6
   c. C-12
   d. A-11

USING A COMMUNITY SERVICES DIRECTORY

Crisis intervention agencies

Department of Health Services Hazardous Waste Hotline
258-6492

Missing Children Hotline
222-3463

Child Abuse Hotline
560-2191 or 344-6000

CRISIS Team
(24 hour counseling service)
236-3339 or 351-0757

Home Run—Runaway Hotline
448-4663

Rape/Domestic Violence Hotline
Center for Women's Studies & Services 233-3088

Turning Point Crisis Center
Hospital Alternative
Mental Health Facility 941-2800

Abuse
Adult Protection Service 236-2121
Battered Women 234-3164
Drug Abuse
MITE, Inc. 440-4801
Narcotics Anonymous 584-1007
Pill Addicts Anonymous 692-1215

Air Pollution
Air Pollution Control 565-6626

Alcoholism
Alanon & Alateen 296-2666
Alcoholics Anonymous 239-1365
Alcoholic Detoxication Center 232-9343
Neighborhood Recovery Center 292-5670

Animals
Animal Control Central County Shelter 236-4250
Animal Control South County Shelter 263-7741
Humane Society 299-7012

Child Care
Children's Home Society Day Care Center 278-7800
Family Day Care Licensing 560-2573
Foster Home Licensing 560-2573
YMCA Child Care Resource Service 275-4800

City Offices
City Information & Assistance 236-5555

Civil Rights
American Civil Liberties Union 232-2121

Consumer Protection Agencies
Better Business Bureau 234-0968
Consumer Credit Counselors 234-4118

Education
County Department of Education 292-3500
Unified School District 298-8126

Employment
Able - Disabled, Inc. 231-5990
Crisis Intervention Center 444-1194
Employment Development Department, State of California 237-7715

Housing
Discrimination Hotline 468-7464

Information and Referral
Government Information Center 293-6030
United Way 292-4777

Legal
Victims of Crime Resource Center 842-8467

Libraries
Law Library 236-2233
City 236-5800
County 565-5100

Marriage Licenses
Court Clerk 236-3197

Medicare
Champus 233-2301
Medi-Cal - Department of Social Services 292-9371
State Disabilities Program 237-7586

Mental Health
County Mental Information & Crisis Counseling 236-3339
Alliance for the Mentally Ill 523-5933
Hotline 236-4903

Missing Children
Kevin Collins Foundation for Missing Children 435-7538
Protect Your Child 276-2350

Parks & Recreation
City 236-5740
County 565-3600
State Park System 237-6770

Postal Service
U.S. Post Office (Main) 221-3310

Professional Referrals
Chiropractic Society Doctors Referral Service 291-5501
Dental Society 223-5391
Lawyers Referral Service 231-8585

POISON CONTROL CENTER—543-6000

Look at the questions on page 177. Talk with another student or a small group of students. Discuss what you would do in each situation. There may be several different ways of trying to find answers for each problem. You may want to look at the names of agencies listed on this page or on previous pages. You may also want to consider other possible solutions.

Share your solutions with the rest of the class. Discuss possible consequences to each solution.

Make a list of other problem situations that you or other students have experienced and discuss alternatives for solving them.

Who Would You Call/What Would You Do

1. If you wanted to find out about child care for your daughter, who would you call?

   _____

2. If you wanted to locate the nearest playground for your children, _____

   _____

3. If your children needed immunizations for school, _____

   _____

4. If your baby drank some furniture polish, _____

   _____

5. If you suspected your child was taking drugs, _____

   _____

6. If your neighbors were beating their child, _____

   _____

7. If you needed an ambulance, _____

   _____

8. If a child were hit by a car in front of your home, _____

   _____

9. If your husband or wife had a drinking problem, _____

   _____

10. If you saw smoke coming from your neighbor's house, _____

    _____

11. If your neighbor threatened to kill himself, _____

    _____

12. If you thought a TV repair company had cheated you, _____

    _____

13. If you wanted to know about the reputation of a business, _____

    _____

14. If you didn't have any money and needed a lawyer, _____

    _____

15. If you were looking for a job, _____

    _____

16. If you wanted to learn a trade to get a job, _____

    _____

17. If you wanted to find out where the nearest elementary school was, _____

    _____

18. If your child ran away from home, _____

    _____

chapter 9

GOVERNMENT AND LAW

COMPETENCY OBJECTIVES

On completion of this unit the students will show orally, in writing, or through demonstration that they are able to use language needed in the following situations:

A. LEGAL AID

- Inquire about one's rights in order to cancel a contract.
- Complain to a landlord in order to get back a cleaning deposit.
- Identify sources of legal help.
- Interpret information about filing a suit in a small claims court.

B. ARREST AND TRIAL IN THE COURTS

- Discuss one's rights when arrested.
- Describe the basic legal process from arrest through trial.
- Define specific types of crimes and identify the courts in which they would be tried.

C. GOVERNMENT AGENCIES

- Interpret a chart on the three levels of government in the U.S.
- Use a telephone directory to locate key federal, state, and local government agencies.
- Discuss the services available through key government agencies in order to solve specific problems.

D. CITIZENSHIP/BASIC RIGHTS

- Discuss the basic requirements for becoming a citizen of the U.S.
- State the basic rights and privileges of citizenship.
- Interpret information about the Bill of Rights and discuss one's rights according to the Bill of Rights.

NEEDS ASSESSMENT EXERCISE ───────────────

GOVERNMENT AND LAW

I need to improve my English so that I can

_____ understand my legal rights to cancel a contract.

_____ understand how to file a complaint with a landlord.

_____ know where to obtain legal help and information.

_____ understand how and when to file a suit in small claims court.

_____ understand a person's rights when arrested.

_____ understand the basic steps from an arrest to a trial (arraignment, trial, jury, verdict, sentencing).

_____ identify the types of courts in the court system.

_____ identify different types of crimes.

_____ understand the requirements to become a citizen of the U.S.

_____ understand the basic rights and privileges of citizenship.

_____ identify an individual's rights according to the Bill of Rights.

_____ use a telephone directory to locate important federal, state, and local government agencies.

_____ understand the different levels of government in the U.S.

THE FREEZER PLAN

A: Hello, my name is Ann Lee. I have a complaint about one of your salespeople. Are you the person to talk with about this problem?

B: Yes, I am. What seems to be the trouble?

A: Two days ago, I signed a contract for your special package plan, the one for a freezer filled with food for only $1,000.

B: Yes.

A: I didn't realize that we'd be paying $600 for a freezer that sells for about $300. Today I called the salesperson back to tell him I wanted to cancel the contract. He said it was too late.

B: I'm sorry, but your contract has already been approved.

A: My neighbor told me that Federal Trade Commission regulations say that I have three days in which to change my mind and cancel my contract.

B: I'm sure there must be some misunderstanding. If you'll give me your name and address, I'll have someone call you.

A: I would appreciate that. If I don't hear from you by tomorrow, I'll have to call my lawyer.

PRACTICE

I didn't realize that we'd be paying $600 for a freezer.
       know

I'm sure there must be some misunderstanding.
               a   mistake.
               an   error.

If I don't hear from you by tomorrow, I'll have to call my lawyer.
                                       I'll have to call the manager.
                                       I'll have to cancel the appointment.
                                       I'll have to sign the contract.

I would appreciate that.
I would like that.
Thank you very much.

INTERVIEW

1. Have you ever signed a contract for anything?
   If yes, did you have any problems with the salespeople?
2. Have you ever changed your mind about a contract that you signed?
   If yes, what happened? What did you do?

A: My landlord certainly isn't keeping the agreement he made.
B: Maybe you need some legal advice on your rights.
   What's the problem?
A: He's never fixed the broken steps, and they're dangerous.
   Besides, his dog keeps frightening my friends.
B: You'd better see a lawyer. The landlord should keep the place up.
   After all, you pay your rent and your taxes.
A: You said it! I've just paid them and am I broke!
   Instead of a lawyer, I'll have to go to Legal Aid.

PRACTICE

His dog keeps frightening my friends.
             barking all night.
             biting people.
             running all over the neighborhood.

Instead of a lawyer, I'll have to go to Legal Aid.
            doctor   a clinic.
            the landlord   the housing office.

The landlord should keep the place up.
                    his agreement.
             fix the broken steps.
             tie his dog up.

The renter should see a lawyer.
             call Legal Aid.
             get renter's insurance.
             move.

INTERVIEW

Have you ever had a problem with your landlord?
What did you do?
What did the landlord do?

SMALL CLAIMS COURT

A: May I speak to the manager?
B: I'm the manager.

A: Yes, this is _____ in apartment 7.
I was wondering when I'll get my cleaning deposit of $200 back,
since I'll be moving out this Friday.
B: I'm sorry, but it's our policy to use that money to clean
the carpeting and drapes when you move out.
A: That's not what I was told when I moved in. I was told
that I would get my deposit back as long as I left the apartment
in the same condition as when I moved in.
B: Sorry, but we have new management now, and that's our policy.
A: But I have it written down on my rental agreement. If you cannot
honor that agreement, I'll have to sue for my deposit
in small claims court.

PRACTICE

I was wondering when I'll get my cleaning deposit back.
　　　　　　　　　　　　　　　　　　refund
　　　　　　　　　　　　　　　　　　tax return

That's not what I was told when I moved in.
　　　　　　　　　　　　　　　　got the job.
　　　　　　　　　　　　　　　　bought the car.
　　　　　　　　　　　　　　　　signed the contract.

I was told that I would _____ as long as I _____ .
　　　　　　　　　　　　　　1　　　　　　　　　　　　　　　2

1. get a refund
　 get a raise
　 get a free ticket
　 get a rebate
　 get a discount

2. kept the receipt
　 performed well on the job
　 sent in the coupon
　 mailed the receipt
　 made a reservation early

Pair Practice: Practice a complaint dialogue like the one in this lesson using the cue words below. Student A begins.

Student A.
1. Two months ago—roof repaired—still leaking
2. Was told—guaranteed for six months
3. Written down—my contract

4. File a claim

Student B.
1. Nothing we can do

2. Sorry

3. Sorry—new ownership of company
4. Have someone call you

INTERVIEW

1. Has anyone ever made an agreement with you about something and then broken the agreement?
2. Have you ever heard of small claims court?
3. Have you ever filed a claim in a small claims court?
   If yes, why did you file the claim?
   Who did you file the claim against?
   What happened in the trial?
   If no, do you know anyone who has ever filed a claim? Describe the case.
4. Do you know what the maximum amount of money is that you can file a claim for in small claims court in your city?
5. If someone cheated you of $500 in your country, and you wanted the money back, how would the problem be solved in your country?

_____ UNDERSTANDING SMALL CLAIMS COURT

INFORMATION FOR THE SMALL CLAIMS PLAINTIFF

This information sheet is written for the person who sues in the small claims court. It explains some of the rules and some general information about the small claims court. It may also be helpful for the person who is sued.

WHAT IS SMALL CLAIMS COURT?

Small claims court is a special court where disputes are resolved quickly and cheaply. The rules are simple and informal. The person who sues is the plaintiff. The person who is sued is the defendant. In small claims court, you may ask a lawyer for advice before you go to court, but you cannot have a lawyer in court. Your claim cannot be for more than $1,500. If you have a claim for more than this amount, you may sue in the regular division of the municipal court or you may sue in the small claims court and give up your right to the amount over $1,500.

Study the information about small claims courts to answer the following questions.

1. What is the maximum amount of money you can sue for in a small claims court?

    a. any amount
    b. $1,500
    c. $2,000
    d. $500

2. Who is the plaintiff in a small claims court?

    a. the person who sues
    b. the person who is sued
    c. the lawyer who represents the one who sues
    d. the clerk who files the claim

3. Which of the following statements is true?

    a. You must pay a lawyer $1,500 to represent you in small claims court.
    b. A lawyer must file the claim for you in small claims court.
    c. A lawyer may not represent you in a small claims court.
    d. The court will appoint a lawyer for you for small claims court.

4. In which of the following situations could you go to small claims court?

    a. You can't pay a traffic ticket.
    b. A car repair shop charged you for repairs that were not made.
    c. You were injured in an accident and had $5,000 in medical bills.
    d. You want to get a divorce.

YOUR RIGHTS WHEN ARRESTED _____

A: You have the right <u>to remain silent</u>.
                              1
B: I have the right to what?
A: You have the right to remain silent.
B: Oh, you mean <u>I don't have to answer your questions</u>?
                              2
A: Yes, that's right.

Pair Practice: Practice the conversation above using the following substitutions. Practice first with your teacher and then with a partner.

1. to give up the right to remain silent, but anything you say can and will be used against you in a court of law
2. I can decide to talk with you, but you can tell the judge and jury what I tell you?

1. to speak with an attorney
2. I can get a lawyer?

1. to have an attorney present during questioning
2. I can have a lawyer with me when you ask me questions?

1. if you so desire, to have an attorney appointed for you without charge
2. If I don't have enough money for a lawyer, you will get one for me and it won't cost me any money?

PRACTICE

Look at the pictures on page 187 while you practice these sentences. First listen to your teacher say each sentence. Then practice with your class, using the substitutions. Can you think of other things to say about each picture?

1. She took some perfume.
      stole
   She didn't pay for the perfume.
   She put the perfume in her purse.
         it

2. The security guard saw her.
                        caught
                        stopped
                        questioned
                        interrogated
                        confronted
                        apprehended

3. The policeman arrested her for shoplifting.
                   put handcuffs on her.
                   handcuffed her.
                   read her her rights.
                   told

4. They took her to the police station.
                 fingerprints.
      fingerprinted her.
   She was fingerprinted.
   She could make one telephone call.
   She was allowed to make one telephone call.

5. They booked her.
   She was booked.
           arraigned.

6. Her parents posted bail.
   She was released on bail.
            freed

7. She was tried in court.
   They tried her in court.
   She had a court trial.
            jury
              trial by jury.
   Her lawyer defended her.
        attorney
   The court prosecuted her.

8. The jury found her guilty
   of the crime.
   She was found guilty.
   The judged sentenced her.
   The judge fined her $500.
   She was fined $500.
           had to pay a $500 fine.

Pair Practice: Practice telling the story above using questions and answers. Practice first with the class and then with a partner. Refer to the pictures on page 187.

EXAMPLE: Student A: What happened? (picture 1)

           Student B: _____ .
           Student A: What happened next?
                            or
                        What happened after she put the perfume in her purse?
           Student B: After she put the perfume in her purse,

                        _____ .

Look at the pictures below and on the next page. Talk about each one. Then write a story about what happened. Make it like a story you might see in the newspaper or hear on the radio or TV. Your story should answer these questions:

What happened?

Who _____ ?

Where _____ ?

When _____ ?

What did _____ do?

What did _____ do after _____ ?

Share your story with the rest of the class. You may want to ask your teacher to help you with some of the legal terms and vocabulary.

1

steal

2

question

3

arrest

4

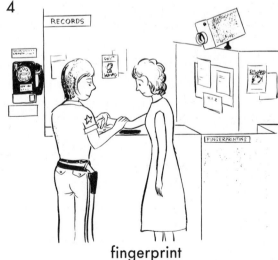

fingerprint

5

book

6

release

7

try

8

sentence

INTERVIEW

If this situation took place in your country, what would happen?
What would be the same?
What would be different?
Do you know anyone who has been arrested in the U.S.?
What happened?
Where can you get help if you are arrested?

MISDEMEANOR CRIMES—minor crimes
Disturbing the peace: Being too noisy in public
Shoplifting: Stealing from a store
FELONY CRIMES—major crimes
Murder: Killing someone
Robbery: Stealing personal property with the use
of violence against another person
Burglary: Breaking and entering a place in order
to steal
Rape: Sexually attacking another person
Child Abuse: Hitting a child and causing injury
Assault: Putting someone in fear of being attacked
Battery: Attacking another person and causing injury
Drug smuggling: Bringing illegal drugs into the U.S.
DWI: Driving while under the influence of alcohol
Counterfeiting: Making false money
Prostitution: Selling sex for money
Extortion: Taking property through a threat to someone
Embezzlement: Stealing money through a business operation
Kidnapping: Stealing children

The following could be felony crimes or misdemeanor crimes:

Burglary, assault, battery, DWI, prostitution.

Pair Practice: Use the information above and the following situations to ask and answer questions.

EXAMPLE: Student A: If <u>someone killed another person</u>, what would he or she be charged with?
Student B: He or she would be charged with murder.

1. Someone killed another person.
2. Someone printed some $100 bills in his house.
3. A man forced a woman to have sex with him.
4. Someone played very loud music until 4:00 in the morning, and the neighbors complained.
5. Someone hit a woman and stole her purse.
6. Someone broke into an empty house and stole a TV.
7. Someone stole a baby from a hospital.
8. Some gang members threatened to kill a restaurant owner if he didn't give them free meals.
9. Someone stole a package of chicken from the grocery store.
10. A woman hit her child and broke the child's arm.

There are three levels of courts: municipal (city) courts, state courts, and federal courts (for United States laws).

Most misdemeanor cases are tried in municipal courts. Other cases, such as those dealing with traffic violations, juvenile crimes, small claims, and family problems, are also tried in the municipal courts. Felony cases involving state laws are tried in the state trial courts.

State trial courts (sometimes called Superior courts)			
Municipal courts			
Family court	Small claims court	Traffic court	Juvenile court

Small Group Activity: Sit in groups of three or four. Take turns asking each other the following questions. Decide in what type of court each case would be heard.

1.   If a 13-year-old boy was arrested for stealing, where would the case be heard?
2.   If someone wanted to get a speeding ticket taken away, where would the case be heard?
3.   If someone killed another person, where would the case be heard?
4.   If someone wanted to sue a car salesperson for $1,000 and didn't want a lawyer, where would the case be heard?
5.   If someone wanted a divorce, where would the case be decided?

INTERVIEW

1.   Have you ever seen a trial on TV?
     What program was it on?
2.   Have you ever been inside a courtroom?
     What type of case was being heard?
     What was the result?

KNOWING THE LEVELS OF GOVERNMENT

	LEGISLATIVE BRANCH (Makes laws)	EXECUTIVE BRANCH (Enforces laws)	JUDICIAL BRANCH (Decides laws)
FEDERAL GOVERNMENT	Congress Senate (100) House of Representatives (435)	President Vice President Cabinet	United States Supreme court Appeals courts District courts
STATE GOVERNMENT	State Legislature Two houses (except Nebraska)	Governor Lieutenant Governor	State Supreme court Appeals courts Trial courts
LOCAL GOVERNMENT COUNTY *(Other)	Board of Supervisors _____	Board of Supervisors or County Commissioner _____	County Courts _____
CITY *(Other)	City Council _____	Mayor City Manager _____	Municipal courts _____

*If the government in your county or city is different, fill in the correct information.

Study the chart on levels of government in the United States to answer the following questions.

1. What branch of government makes laws?
    a. The executive branch
    b. The judicial branch
    c. The legislative branch

2. What does the judicial branch do?
    a. Decides laws
    b. Makes laws
    c. Enforces laws

3. Who enforces the laws at the state level?
    a. The President
    b. The state legislature
    c. The governor

4. Who makes the laws at the federal level?
    a. The President
    b. The Congress
    d. The Cabinet

5. Who decides the laws at the city level?
    a. The Supreme Court
    b. The appeals courts
    c. The municipal courts

6. What is the highest court at the federal level?
    a. The district court
    b. The State Supreme court
    c. The U.S. Supreme court

7. What does the President of the U.S. do?
    a. He decides federal laws.
    b. He enforces federal laws.
    c. He makes all laws.

8. How many houses are there in the Congress?
    a. 1
    b. 2
    c. 3

9. What does a mayor do?
    a. A mayor enforces the laws in the city.
    b. A mayor makes the laws for the state.
    c. A mayor decides the laws for the city.

10. How many senators are there in the Congress?
    a. 435
    b. 100
    c. 2

Pair Practice: Practice asking and answering questions with the following pattern. The correct answer is in parentheses so that you can check your partner's answer.

What does _____ do?

What do _____ do?

EXAMPLE: Student A: What does Congress do?
               Student B: Congress makes the laws at the federal level.
               Student A: (Look at the answer in the list below.)
                              Yes, that's right.

A

1. Congress
   (makes the laws at the federal level)
2. Governor
   (enforces laws—state level)
3. State Supreme court
   (decides laws—state level)
4. Municipal courts
   (decide laws—local level)

B

1. President
   (enforces the laws—federal)
2. City council
   (makes laws—local level)
3. State legislature
   (makes laws—state)
4. District courts
   (decide laws—federal level)

LOCATING GOVERNMENT AGENCIES

In the telephone directory, there are listings for federal (U.S.), state, and city government agencies. Each section gives numbers to call for services and information or to get answers to questions and solve problems.

Below are sample listings from each section. Study them carefully. Then try to answer the questions on the next page.

United States Government Offices

Civil Service Commission	293-6165
Equal Employment Opportunity	557-6288
FBI	231-1122
Federal Job Information Center	293-6165
Immigration & Naturalization	557-5570
Internal Revenue Service	800-242-4585

State Government Offices

Employment Development	
Employment Service	237-7715
Unemployment Claims	237-7711
Fire Marshall	237-7216
Fish & Game Department	237-7311
Highway Condition Information	293-3484

County Government Offices

Adult Abuse Hotline	560-2118
Animal Control	236-4250
Health Department	
Birth & Death Registration	236-2296
Child Health & Disability	236-3787
Drug Program	236-2200
Family Planning	236-2198
Immunizations	236-2264
WIC—Women, Infants, & Children	531-6119
Emergency Medical Service	236-3259
Information for County Offices	236-2121
Jail	236-3011
Juvenile Hall	560-3500
Public Welfare Department	292-9371
Refuse Disposal—Dumps	565-5818
Road and Street Emergencies	
County	565-5251
after 5 P.M. & holidays	565-5261
Sheriff's Department	236-3111
or dial	Operator
Labor Department	
Occupational Safety & Health	569-9071
Postal Service	
Information	574-0477
Claims	221-2297

Social Security Administration	238-1800
Highway Patrol	283-6365
Industrial Relations	
Industrial Accidents	237-7983
Worker's Compensation	237-7321
Labor Standards	237-7334
Motor Vehicle Department	297-3511

City Government Offices

Consumer Fraud Unit	236-6007
Fire Department	
to report a fire	238-1212
Government Information Center	293-6030
Housing Commission	231-9400
Information for City Offices	236-5555
Library—Central	236-5800
Lights	
Street Lights	236-5505
Traffic Signals	236-5505
Noise Abatement	236-7151
Park & Recreation Department	236-5740
Police Department	
Emergency Calls	911
24-Hour Non-Emergency calls	531-2000
General Information	531-2000
Information related to	
Auto Theft	531-2559
Crime Prevention	531-2672
Traffic	531-2280
Refuse Collection	236-5660
Street Maintenance	
Cleaning & Sweeping	236-5656
Repairs	
Storm Drainage	236-5656
Street Lights	236-5505
Utilities Department	
Emergencies Water & Sewer	236-5600
Turn-on and Shut-off	236-6380
Billing Information	236-6380

Find the telephone number you would call to get information about each of the following. Tell whether it is a federal, state, county, or city agency.

1. Social Security card
2. U.S. citizenship
3. Income taxes
4. Jobs
5. Welfare
6. Local swimming pools
7. Lost mail

8. Trash collection
9. Driver's license
10. Broken water main
11. Traffic light out
12. Unsafe working conditions
13. Dog running loose
14. Books on tape

INTERVIEW

What number would you call in your city to get information on each of the above? Use your local telephone directory to find out. What would you say when you called? Practice these conversations with a partner, and then share them with the rest of the class.

Which of these government services have you used? Have you been able to get the help you needed?

A: Where were you yesterday? We missed you.
B: I took my citizenship test.
A: Citizenship test? Have you been here that long?
B: Yes, I've had my green card for five years.
A: Did you pass?
B: Yes, finally. I had failed the first time, so I was really nervous.
A: That's great. What kind of test was it?
B: It was an oral test. The instructor asked me about 15 questions.
A: Did you know all of them?
B: All of them, except one. The instructor asked me who the chief justice of the Supreme Court was, and I forgot his name.
A: Oh, don't worry. I bet most Americans don't know that either. Congratulations.
B: Thanks.

PRACTICE

What kind of test was it?
It was an oral test.
      a listening
      a written
      a multiple choice
      a true false
      an essay

INTERVIEW

1. Have you ever taken the citizenship test?
   If yes, did you pass it?
   What did they ask you?

2. What other tests have you taken since you came to the U.S.?
   What kinds of tests were they?
   How did you do?

3. How do you feel when you have to take a test?

4. In your country, do you have to take a test to

         become a citizen?
         get a driver's license?
         go to college?
         get a job?

5. What other tests do you have to take in your country?

RIGHTS AND REQUIREMENTS OF CITIZENSHIP

RIGHTS OF CITIZENS

A citizen is a person who is a full member of the U.S. He/she owes loyalty or allegiance to his/her country.

Naturalized citizens can obtain federal government jobs (including those that require a security clearance), can travel with a U.S. passport, and can petition for close relatives to come to the U.S. to live. People who are not citizens do not have these rights. They do not receive all available benefits and are not eligible for all jobs.

Right to Vote

The most important right citizens have is the right to vote.

ELIGIBILITY REQUIREMENTS FOR CITIZENSHIP

To become a citizen, or to be naturalized, a person or applicant must meet certain requirements:
- be at least 18 years old.
- have lived in the U.S. as a legal resident for at least 5 years; must not live out of the U.S. for 30 months or more during the 5-year period;
- be of good moral character and loyal to the U.S.;
- be able to read, write, speak and understand basic English;
- have basic knowledge and understanding of the history, government structure and the Constitution of the U.S.; and,
- be willing to take an oath of allegiance to the U.S.

Study the above paragraph on citizenship (taken from *Citizenship Education and Naturalization Information*, published by the Immigration and Naturalization Service) to decide if the following statements are true or false.

_____ 1. Everyone has to become a citizen of the U.S. after five years of residence.

_____ 2. You must be able to read, write, speak, and understand English to become a citizen.

_____ 3. You must have lived in the U.S. for at least five years as a legal resident.

_____ 4. You cannot become a citizen if you lived outside the U.S. for more than 30 days during the 5-year period.

_____ 5. You have the right to vote in the U.S. if you are a legal resident.

_____ 6. You must be a citizen to bring close relatives to the U.S. to live as residents.

_____ 7. Legal residents are eligible for all jobs in the U.S.

The Bill of Rights

The Bill of Rights is the first 10 amendments or changes to the U.S. Constitution. They were added to the Constitution in 1791. The writers of the Constitution were worried that the Constitution did not protect the freedoms of the people enough, so they added these changes. These rights belong to all people in the United States, citizens and noncitizens.

Amendment 1: Guarantees the freedom of speech, press, assembly, religion, and petition.

Amendment 2: Guarantees the right to have weapons.

Amendment 3: Prevents the government from forcing citizens to keep soldiers in their homes during war or peacetime.

Amendment 4: Prevents the government from searching one's home or private property without permission from the court.

Amendment 5: Guarantees a fair trial for someone accused of a crime. Guarantees a person's right to silence during a trial. Guarantees a person's right to have a lawyer during a trial.

Amendment 6: Guarantees a speedy trial.

Amendment 7: Guarantees a jury trial.

Amendment 8: Prevents cruel or unusual punishment if someone is convicted of a crime.

Amendment 9: Guarantees the people all rights not listed in the Constitution.

Amendment 10: Says rights not given to the federal government belong to the states or people.

Pair Practice: Practice the following questions and answers. Student A asks the questions below and Student B refers to the amendments above to answer the questions.

EXAMPLE: Student A: Do I have the right to attend any church I want to?
            Student B: Yes, you have the right to attend any church you want to according to amendment one.

1.   attend any church I want to
2.   have a gun in my house
3.   sign a petition to change a law
4.   buy a red car
5.   write a letter to the newspaper disagreeing with the President of the U.S.
6.   go to a meeting of the Communist party
7.   not answer a police officer's questions about a crime
8.   paint my house purple
9.   have a lawyer in a trial
10. stop a police officer from looking around my house if he or she doesn't have a reason

CHAPTER 1

Topic: Introductions

1. Divide the class into groups of 3. Have one person in the group introduce the other two. Provide tape recorders for those who wish to hear themselves.

Topic: Polite Expressions

1. Role play similar situations in which the expressions used in the visual would be appropriate (page 1–10).
2. Discuss formal and informal ways of apologizing, expressing thanks to one's boss, teacher, casual friend, close friend, etc.

Topic: Telephone Communications

1. Have students exchange phone numbers and practice calling each other at home (partners must not speak the same native language).
2. Have students practice calling a number which answers with a taped message and then bring information back to class (for example, Tel Med, movie theaters, etc.).

CHAPTER 2

Topic: Supermarket ad

1. Have the students compare the prices in the ad with current local prices. Are local food prices higher or lower than the prices in the ad?
2. Compare what is offered in the supermarkets in the U.S. with that in each student's native country. Are the same food items available? How do prices compare?

Topic: Shopping for food

1. Have the students write short shopping lists which they will exchange with one another. Appoint clerks and cashiers. Using these lists, play money, and food items, have the students role play the shopping trip.
2. Plan a field trip to a local supermarket. Assign students tasks such as getting prices on certain items or purchasing items needed for a food preparation project in class (as long as students are not financially responsible for the purchases).
3. Teach cooking vocabulary and cooking terms through preparing a simple recipe in class, i.e. tuna salad. After demonstrating the steps, elicit the language again in order to do a language experience exercise in writing down the recipe. On subsequent days, ask other students to share recipes, orally first, followed by a language experience exercise, facilitated by the teacher.

Topic: Eating Out

1. Using the menu visuals or menus obtained from local restaurants, have students role play ordering food in a restaurant. You may want to begin with a fast food type restaurant and later advance to a more formal type. If possible, use play money so that paying the bill and tipping can also be practiced.

2. Bring in examples of different types of American salad dressings. Let the students taste and role play ordering the kind of dressing they would like.

CHAPTER 3

Topic: Obtaining medical care

1. Have students role play calling a doctor's or a dentist's office, to make an appointment.
2. Have students get information about the hospitals and/or clinics nearest them: telephone numbers, services, etc.
3. Discuss types and costs of health insurance. Have students call individual companies for information and compare coverage.

Topic: Medications

1. Bring in a pill bottle, cough medicine, a teaspoon and an eyedrop container. Have students role play giving instructions to each other.
2. Discuss buying drugs by their generic names rather than their brand names.
3. Discuss over-the-counter drugs and their possible uses. Compare with prescription drugs. Visit a local drug store and assign students tasks such as getting prices on certain items.

Topic: Emergencies

1. Give emergency telephone number cards to students. Have them look up the local numbers and post them on their telephones at home.
2. Bring in empty containers for poisonous substances. Discuss the directions on the labels, particularly vocabulary terms of warning.
3. Discuss items that should be included in a first aid kit and their uses: aspirin, disinfectants, bandages, etc. Bring in a sample kit.
4. Arrange to have a guest speaker from a local Red Cross agency visit your class to demonstrate emergency procedures.

CHAPTER 4

Topic: Directions

1. Have students practice giving each other directions from school to 1) their homes, 2) local stores, 3) the closest bus stop, etc. Also have them practice writing down directions given by others.

Topic: Bus, Plane, Train schedules

1. Have students use the local directory to look up numbers of the out of town bus station, airport, and train station. Assign students the task of calling to get the rates for each type of transportation to the same destination to compare the prices and time of travel.

2. Have students plan a field trip using the local bus for transportation. They should determine the schedule, the route, and compute fares and total costs.

Topic: *Using the car*

1. Have students role play instructing each other in the operation of a car. Use parts of the car in the instructions. (i.e. put the key in the ignition, turn on the ignition while you step on the gas).
2. Have students role play situations involving receiving a traffic ticket, and service station visits involving various problems with a car.
3. Duplicate used car ads from the local newspaper. Have students study the ads in groups and decide which car they would like to buy and why.
4. Have the students use the yellow pages in the phone book to look up numbers for various car services, i.e. auto parts, headlight adjustment, smog check locations, etc.
5. Discuss the purpose and need for automobile insurance. Have students call different agencies to compare the rates and types of coverage.

CHAPTER 5

Topic: *Housing repairs*

1. Using the visual of "Housing repairs," have students ask and respond to the following:

   A. What do you want to have done?

   B. I want to have the _____ fixed (repaired, etc.)

   A. Who will you have do it?

   B. I'll have a _____ do _____ .

   Have students share what they have had done to their houses or apartments.
2. Have students role play communicating maintenance problems to housing managers and making arrangements for repair.

Topic: *Locating housing*

1. Have students write original want ads on 3 × 5 cards. Put their names on the back of their cards and post the cards on the bulletin board. Then have the students take turns choosing an apartment or house they would like to rent, and discuss rental arrangements with the authors of the ads who act as the managers.
2. Discuss resources available locally to assist the public in locating housing.
3. Discuss the advantages and disadvantages of renting and buying.
4. Discuss rental arrangements students in class have. It's easy to chart the information on the board. Compare the average rents, service charges, regulations, deposits, etc.

CHAPTER 6

Topic: *Clothing*

1. Have students discuss differences and similarities in styles of clothing and fabrics used in the U.S. and in other countries.

2. Have one student describe what another student is wearing; have the other students try to guess who is being described.

Topic: *Clothing care*

1. Bring samples of as many different fabrics as possible. Discuss what each is, how it should be cleaned, and reasons for any special care.
2. Bring samples of clothing that have clothing care labels and assign students tasks to interpret the directions on the labels.

Topic: *Banking*

1. Have students call various banks to obtain local information about interest rates, and savings and checking account plans. Report information to the class and make comparisons.
2. Take a field trip to a local bank or have a speaker come in to discuss banking services.
3. Duplicate blank checks, deposit slips, and withdrawal slips and have students role play bank transactions, filling out the appropriate forms.

CHAPTER 7

Topic: *Looking for a Job*

1. Have the students discuss local alternatives available for obtaining information about jobs, i.e. want ads, friends, local, state, and federal agencies, etc. Look up addresses and telephone numbers.
2. Duplicate employment ads from a local newspaper. Divide students into groups and have them get specific information from the ads and then share with the class. Have students role play making telephone calls to set up appointments for an interview for the job openings indicated.
3. Have students write their own ads seeking employment. Discuss the cost of ads and procedures for getting them published in local newspapers.
4. Have students practice writing their own personal data sheets. Have students then practice completing a variety of different job application forms and writing letters of application.
5. Have students role play simulated job interviews. Video tape interviews and critique, if possible.

Topic: *Keeping a job*

1. Assign groups of students clerical work projects in order to simulate a work situation in which students must ask for clarification and respond to questions about progress, etc. The work projects may assist the school's clerical staff with jobs they need to have done for the school, i.e. collating and stapling.

CHAPTER 8

Topic: *Post Office*

1. Obtain forms from the local post office and have students practice filling them out while they are role playing any of the following situations:

   a) Insuring a package

   b) Registering $1000

    c)   Getting a post office box

    d)   Getting an international money order

    e)   Tracing a lost package

2. Take a field trip to a nearby post office

Topic: Library

1. Have the students list the library services available at local main and branch libraries.

2. Take a field trip to the local library.

Topic: Schools

1. Have the students list educational institutions in the local area and discuss services and training available through each. Obtain schedules and review enrollment procedures and prerequisites.

2. Have the students role play enrolling a child in school and a parent/teacher conference.

Topic: Community Agencies

1. Have the students obtain a map of the local area, and ask them to locate key community agencies, i.e. hospital, schools, airport, etc.

2. Have the students locate cultural and recreation facilities in the area and discuss what each has to offer including prices, schedules, etc. Groups of students could be assigned different attractions to research.

3. Have the students make a list of possible problem situations. Assign each group a problem and assign the group the task of finding out where to go for assistance in solving the problem. Share the information with the class.

CHAPTER 9

Topic: Arrest and Trial

1. Invite a police officer to the class to demonstrate the Miranda warning.

2. Take a field trip to the local courthouse to observe a trial.

Topic: Legal aid

1. Invite a speaker to describe the services of legal aid offices.

Index of Grammar Structures
BY CHAPTER

STRUCTURE	1	2	3	4	5	6	7	8	9
WH-questions	X	X		X	X		X		
There is/are		X							
Count/Non-count nouns		X							
Prepositions of Location	X			X			X		
Conjunctions: *either . . . or*				X					
Imperatives				X					
Past Tense		X							
Future Tense with *going to*			X						
Modals:									
May	X	X			X				
Might			X	X			X		
Can	X				X				
Could					X		X		
Would	X	X		X					
Should		X	X						
Must/Have to		X	X		X				X
Past Tense Modals		X						X	
Comparative		X				X			
Superlative		X							
Past Continuous Tense			X	X					
Present Perfect Tense	X		X		X		X		
Present Perfect Continuous	X						X		
Adverbs						X			
Adverb Clauses			X	X	X		X	X	
Adjective Phrases, Adjective Clauses						X			
Noun Clauses									X
Embedded Questions/Embedded Clauses	X			X			X		X
Reported Speech			X		X		X		X
Present Real Conditional				X	X	X	X		X
Present Unreal Conditional						X		X	X
Tag Questions						X			
Negative Questions						X			
Passive Voice					X			X	X
Gerunds/Infinitives			X	X			X	X	X
Supposed to Pattern						X			
Used to Pattern							X		
Separable Two-Word Verbs								X	
Causals with *have/get*				X	X				